Nails from Bullets

Nails from Bullets

A Soldier's Story of Redemption

Glenn Goree

RESOURCE Publications · Eugene, Oregon

NAILS FROM BULLETS
A Soldier's Story of Redemption

Copyright © 2016 Glenn Goree. All rights reserved. Except for brief quotations in critical publications or reviews, no part of this book may be reproduced in any manner without prior written permission from the publisher. Write: Permissions, Wipf and Stock Publishers, 199 W. 8th Ave., Suite 3, Eugene, OR 97401.

Scripture is taken from the holy Bible, New International VersionÒ. NIVÒ. CopyrightÓ 1973, 1978, 1984 by International Bible Society. Used by permission of Zondervan. All rights reserved worldwide.

Resource Publications
An Imprint of Wipf and Stock Publishers
199 W. 8th Ave., Suite 3
Eugene, OR 97401

www.wipfandstock.com

PAPERBACK ISBN: 978-1-4982-9833-9
HARDCOVER ISBN: 978-1-4982-4886-0
EBOOK ISBN: 978-1-4982-9834-6

Manufactured in the U.S.A.   JUNE 29, 2016

This book is dedicated to all the men and women of the American Armed Forces who have paid the ultimate price for the freedom of our country.

Contents

Introduction | ix
Poem: Nails from Bullets | 1

1. The Knife | 3
2. The Terrorist's Death | 10
3. The Terrorist's Conversation with God | 13
4. The Medic | 20
5. The Red Helicopter | 25
6. Nails from Bullets | 32
7. Ascension | 40
8. Grace | 43
9. The Choice | 47
10. Prelude | 49
11. Copilot | 56
12. Orientation to Death and Hades | 61
13. How to Use Your Swords to Capture Souls | 76
14. Advanced Class on Winning Souls for Satan | 97
15. Man Prefers a Complicated Lie Over the Simple Truth | 102
16. Comfort, Convenience, Complacency, and Indifference | 116
17. How to Win Adolescent Souls | 123
18. Sky Pilot | 128
19. The Water of Life | 135
20. The Fog of War | 140

Epilogue | 144

Introduction

Warriors, you gave it all. You also left bits and pieces of your hearts and souls on the battlefield. In some ways, you died on the field, and have no desire to ever return. You thought your innocence was lost during boot camp or basic training. But you soon learned your initial introduction to the military was only the beginning. You also learned no matter how tough your training was, nothing could prepare you for death and dying on the battlefield. Preparing for war is an arduous task, but the training doesn't come close to enduring a battle firsthand.

The best military in the world prepared you for combat. You entered the armed services with lofty ideals, or perhaps a friend talked you into in to joining. Maybe you weren't ready for college or university. Or maybe you were like a friend of mine during the Vietnam War era. He got a girl pregnant during the last few months of our senior year in high school. He discovered the Army was his temporary haven to avoid conjugal accountability.

Initially, the altruistic ideals of serving God and country convinced you to sign up to fight. But once a shower of bullets whizzed past your head and others kicked dirt up into your eyes, your motive to survive grew within you. Soon, God and country took second place. Survival became a day-by-day experience, or sometimes an hour-by-hour achievement.

Now that you're home, what do you do with all those memories? Where do you store them so they stay buried forever? Why is it you can't find that vault in your deep subconscious to house

Introduction

them? Why can't you close the door, lock it, and throw away the key? No matter how hard you try, the memoires keep resurfacing. They continue to find some way to unlock the door and break out into your conscious mind. At night you can't sleep because in your nightmares those images cause cold sweats, crying. Maybe even unknowingly, you attack your spouse.

Irritability, argumentative, sullen, quiet, can't keep a job, alcohol or drug abuse, affairs, infidelity, divorce. These symptoms either plague your life or drag you down. Counseling? You're not going down that road. Why should you pay a hundred dollars or more an hour to see some counselor who has never been in the military, much less seen any combat? How could he or she know anything about the ordeals you faced, and still relive on a nightly basis? All they do is give you a diagnosis, slip you some pills, and call you a *patient*. Who needs treatment? Veterans need help not treatment.

Nails from Bullets employs the styles used in *The Screwtape Letters* by C. S. Lewis, *God Have Mercy on Us*, by William T. Scanion, published in 1929, and *Company K* by William E. Campbell, published in 1933. This may seem like an unusual combination, but let me explain.

God Have Mercy on Us is the story of the writer when he served as a Marine, from the Battle of Belleau Woods, 6 June, 1918, until the Armistice, 11 November, 1918. William T. Scanion not only reveals The Great War's brutality, but he tells the human side of the warrior. His revelation of personal thoughts is limited to a commentary of what the warriors felt about their present life-and-death struggles. In these brief eye-openers, he does not stray into their personal lives.

Company K was written about individual Marines who fought in WW I. Each chapter bears a man's name instead of a number. The short stories represent true events, although the names of some of the soldiers were changed to protect their identities. William Campbell pulled no punches. The reader is not shielded from encountering the suffering and pain in The Great War. However, none of the stories delves into personal feelings or emotions.

Introduction

The Screwtape Letters, on the other hand, is a satire. In this work, Lewis explores life, both living and demonic, in this world and the next. His work investigates the psyche by peeling away the layers of onion—life, to get down to the center of the soul. You cannot read his work without seeing yourself, and then wishing that you'd never opened the book. Lewis has a way of showing us who and what we really are.

I have attempted to tie the themes from these three books together. Like braiding the three to form one smooth rope. I'm not only going to offer the reader true-life battle experiences which lead to Post-Traumatic Stress Disorder, but also include what warriors are *thinking* and *feeling*, and how these raw emotions contribute to PTSDw. In the end, I believe PTSD is more a spiritual ailment than a psychological condition.

War is not one dimensional. It is comprised of three levels—heaven, hell, and the battlefield. Hence, after many years of counseling clients with PTSD, I have used those experiences to address the spiritual side of war. This book confronts the eternal conflict between heaven and hell. I must emphasize that this battle for souls does not take a hiatus in war. If anything, Satan enhances his army's training to capitalize on the evil of mortal combat. As pointed out in this book, Satan's minions are after every soul, at any cost. To increase the stakes, they are not constrained by time since they are already dead. Their best strategy is to use war's evil impact on the psyche of the soul. The devastating pain war causes makes a soldier more vulnerable.

But what is hell? What does it look like? What do souls experience while waiting there until Christ's return? The most important question—how does Satan train his troops to capture souls?

Here is where a theme in C.S. Lewis's *Screwtape Letters* guided my imagination. In order to answer these four vital questions, I placed myself in what I believe is a facsimile of hell. Some readers may dispute my written visitation into the evil unknown because it does not follow traditional interpretation. I welcome your comments, complementary or derogatory. If a reader is stirred enough to comment, then this book's mission has been accomplished.

Introduction

Naturally, there is no record of dialogue between a senior and junior demon on how best to catch souls. However, many people believe that Satan will exploit mortal weaknesses in order to recruit souls for his eternal domain.

The goal of this book is to aid in the healing of PTSD. Men and women returning home from war often have tortured souls. They saw Satan and God on the battlefield every day. Not literally of course, but in the acts of fellow comrades in arms and the enemy. Ironically, the actual enemy is Satan. He is responsible for the evil they witnessed, while God is behind the sacrifice and love observed.

Returning warriors also suffer from a spiritual source of guilt. Their souls and core beliefs are shaken and tested during combat. It's in this context I offer the tools and tactics Satan uses to snare them. Of course, Satan also uses these tactics to nab civilians for his kingdom. The ultimate goal of this book is to offer help to soldiers, civilians, and their families in their spiritual war against Satan on the battlefield of life.

Nails from Bullets

Nails from bullets.
Strange words for military pundits!

But this solution is desperately needed
For our warriors whose pain has been excessively exceeded.

Who will listen to the noble call
Of warriors returning home who gave it all?

Who will honor that they stand straight and tall,
Because they fought and defeated tyranny's chain and ball?

Did they not pay the ultimate price,
So that you and I could sleep at home, comfortably nice?

Were their lives not riveted each day
When, like dice, Satan threw them into combat's fray?

No, they didn't sacrifice their mortal lives.
But they gave even more to what war contrives.

For, you see, they lost bits and pieces of their souls
Every time they, in terror, had to hide in mother earth's
dank, dark holes.

They lived as though deceased each day and night,
Having to fight and survive, yet watch brothers they loved die in
fright.

So what are these nails and from where do they come?
They're found in a cross upon which our Savior died
when His work was done!

Nails from Bullets

Nails from bullets is what they need
To sooth and heal their wounds of war's dark deeds.

For in Christ alone they weep and mourn,
Because they suffered what few souls have borne.

Nails from bullets is the only way,
Because they have a Savior who personally knows how their hearts pay!

> "The race is not to the swift or the battle to the strong."
>
> ECCL 9:11

1

The Knife

Dereck, the Rhodesian Light Infantry soldier, rubbed his bare arms. He couldn't talk out loud, so his thoughts pounded in his brain.

The night air was freezing. How could it be so hot by day and freezing at night? Sweat-soaked khakis makes it harder to stay warm after the sun goes down. Sunburned arms, and the back of his neck and legs didn't help, either.

Pitch black. Even if he stuck his arm straight out in front, he couldn't see his hand.

Darn this thick bush. No matter how he tried to move quietly, there was always something to step on step over.

Twigs, dried leaves, and the darn vines and branches all made a racket.

Slowly, move slowly. Carefully place one foot at a time. Heal down, then gently place the rest of the foot in a rolling motion.

The rest of his squad was to his right. Confidence in their abilities boosted his spirit.

Stop! What's that noise? It's something big. Freeze!

Nails from Bullets

Fear raged through his chest and sent adrenalin pumping into his bloodstream.

Banza, the freedom fighter or terrorist, depending on your frame of reference, stopped dead in his tracks.

Stand still. Perfectly still. Don't even breathe.

Several minutes ticked by. Who knew how long? Seemed like an eternity.

OK, now let your breath out very slowly, but darn you, keep still!

Like his opponent, Banza recalled his training. Stay alive.

He didn't hear another sound. Probably just some small animal, he hoped.

Splat.

Why did he swat that mosquito? He knew better. A noise like that carried a mile in the bush on the still night air.

Tired. I'm so very tired. My muscles ache. I wish I could lie down and go to sleep.

Running all day playing cat and mouse with the white soldier had sapped his energy. He could probably sleep all day and still not be rested.

Banza had told his group leader to prepare a more careful ambush, but the man hadn't listened. Now they were all dead. If the team leader was alive right this very moment, Banza would beat him to a pulp.

The RLI—Rhodesian Light Infantry patrol had been tracking him all day. His AK rifle was useless. Ran out of shells hours ago. All he had was his knife. And his wits.

Yes, I will be all right. I won't lose my life tonight.

Discipline. He remembered the bush discipline. Okay. Lift your leg and foot slowly. Doesn't matter how tired you are. Rather be tired than dead. Move slowly. Carefully.

He heard nothing now. Not even the breeze rustling the leaves. Those RLI guys were amateurs. They wouldn't find him.

Darn! The blister on his heel must be an inch deep.

The Knife

Blasted Quarter Master. Banza had told him he needed a different pair of boots. The man wouldn't listen. Take them or leave them, he'd said. Well, if or when Banza returned to base, he'd kill him.

Fatigue. Exhaustion. Banza had never been this tired before.

War was not like the game of soccer where everybody shook hands at the end of the game, and went home to rest. In this arena, there was only the winner and the dead.

Dereck sniffed like an old hunting dog searching for its quarry. *What's that smell?*

In the same instant, Banza drew in a deep breath. *There's a soldier close by.* He slowly knelt and placed his AK 47 down as quietly as he could, and then eased his knife out of its sheathe.

Whites all smell alike. I know one of them is near my position. Banza's body tensed like a lion just moments before it pounced on its next meal.

With a smirk, Dereck cocked his head. *Blacks have an unmistakable stench. Oh, God what a terrible smell. Intense body odor mingled with campfire smoke.*

Slowly he raised his FN rifle but instead of bracing it on his shoulder, he placed the butt between his arm and his body. His finger curled tighter around the trigger. He needed to squeeze and not pull the trigger, but in close quarters, any shot that left him alive and the terrorist dead, was all that mattered.

Then he paused to sniff the air without making a sound, because even the sucking of air through his nose could give him away.

Free of his AK 47, Banza raised his knife slowly with his left hand. First, to waist height then to chest level while gripping the handle tighter and tighter. *Yes, that feels right. No anxiety, no fear.* He held extended his right arm, with a slight bend at the elbow. Poised now, like the stinger on a scorpion.

Banza imitated the leopard, knees slightly bent, torso about to explode with energy. Then it occurred to him perhaps he should bend down just a few inches lower. It would make him less of a target. So he bent his knees to just shy of a squatting position.

Instinct kicked in. His white adversary was only a few feet away.

Dereck's intuition rang like the Liberty Bell in his head. *He's close. Darn bush. Can't see a thing.*

A twig snapped.

Both opponents sucked in air. They were determined to kill each other.

No one else would have heard the twig snap. However, these two heard it as though a logger chopped down an oak tree.

Banza searched the sky for any light. A sliver of moon peeked out from the clouds. Just for a moment, as a cloud sluggishly drifted past the moon, a ray of light revealed his would-be killer less than a foot away.

Has he seen me?

Idiot. He's going to die for breaking that twig.

He tensed as he prepared to thrust his knife forward into the soldier's body.

Dereck berated himself. *Fool. Why'd you break that twig?* He mentally regrouped and focused. *I can smell him but I can't see him.*

While the brief light from the moon momentarily acted like a flashlight, he searched the vicinity, but the terrorist was nowhere in sight.

Standing as still as a statue, Dereck froze. Never mind mosquitos were feasting on his bare skin.

What was that? A breath, a knee joint creaking? Someone or something moved to his right.

Dereck turned his head, but not soon enough. The blade of a knife sliced into his side, just missing his ribs.

Darn. Banza realized his knife missed its mark. As quickly as he thrust the knife forward the first time, he drew it back, and thrust a second time.

Too late.

Mistakes in this type of warfare were fatal.

The Knife

As if on cue, the clouds exposed the moon just long enough so the combatants could see each other.

Banza saw the soldier aim his rifle toward him. But he blocked the FN with his right forearm, pushing the hot barrel that was spitting slugs of death. The hot barrel burned his hand, but he ignored the pain.

He had to retaliate. Banza thrust his knife a second time. The soldier was close enough he could smell the man's offensive body odor. The knife would do serious damage this time. But as Banza lunged forward, he slipped. He regained his footing but he was at a disadvantage as he staggered erect.

Dereck took advantage of the terrorist's mistake. He screamed, "I'm gonna kill you, black man, and then I'm gonna cut your balls off as a trophy. You think you can kill me?"

Demonic rage empowered Dereck as he threw his FN down, then grabbed for the terrorist's knife. He didn't want to shoot the terrorist now. Instead, he had an insane desire to feel the knife pierce his body and sink home into as many internal organs as possible.

Both men were weak from lack of food, from fatigue, and most of all, from dehydration.

They were now locked in face-to-face, body-to-body warfare as they wrestled and rolled around in the bush. Each man grappled for control of the knife. They kicked each other, and gouged out hunks of flesh as they clawed like leopards. Soon, they realized they could use their teeth too, just like the lion. They gnawed at each other. What do they bite? Anything they could sink their teeth into.

A primordial howl.

"You bit off my ear." Blood flowed from Dereck's right ear, gushing like a river.

Then Banza hollered in his native MaShona tongue, "You white bastard." With his left hand, he reached up to his nose. It was gone. Blood poured down into his mouth. He choked and gagged as his lungs searched for air.

Nails from Bullets

Now both men were at an equal disadvantage with body parts missing, and loosing blood.

Salt from their body fluids stung their eyes. Their struggle was so intense, sweat covered their bodies, making them slippery. Neither man could secure a firm hold on his opponent to either break his neck, or strangle him until there was no more oxygen for his brain.

This struggle was nothing like you'd see in Hollywood movies, or on TV shows. There wouldn't be one solid karate chop with the side of the hand, or punishing kick, to end the fight.

Banza tried to take advantage of the wound he inflicted with the knife, and smashed his fist into the bloody gash.

In agony, Dereck let out a blood-curdling roar.

Then Banza tore away flesh with his finger nails.

Dereck bellowed like a wounded animal.

For a few moments, Banza thought he's going to gain the upper hand. What he didn't take into consideration was that the soldier had become a deadly beast.

Finally, Dereck yanked the knife out of the terrorist's left hand. He managed to straddle his enemy, with his knee smashing down on the man's arms.

In a perfect position to strike, Dereck plunged the knife deep into the terrorist's chest. A satanic rage empowered him.

The battle was more than two enemies fighting to the death. There was vengeance in the blade. There was rage in the thrust. There was an unmerciful darkness in the eyes of the soldier.

Like a victorious gladiator in the Roman Arena, the soldier yelled, "See gook. I got ya." To celebrate his victory, Dereck beat his chest like a male gorilla.

True to his promise, he castrated his opponent. "You're dead now. You won't hurt anyone ever again."

With a sigh, Dereck picked up his FN. Then he searched the corpse for souvenirs. Of course he took the knife, and then he rummaged in the man's pockets for any information he could pass on to the Intelligence Department. Nothing.

The Knife

When Dereck's mates heard his FN firing, several come to his aid. But when they arrived, they realized he didn't need their help. Without a sound, they all disappeared into the bush as quickly as they had appeared. They became like a vanishing mist, or smoke from a fire. No time for celebration, especially if they wanted to stay alive. No time to render medical care to Dereck. He could walk. First aid would have to wait until they reached a place of safety. They weren't sure who else was out in the bush, and couldn't risk the chance of being ambushed. They disappeared like a fading shadow.

> "The Lord is not slow in keeping his promise, as some understand slowness. He is patient with you, not wanting anyone to perish, but everyone to come to repentance."
>
> II PET 3:9

2

The Terrorist's Death

In those last few moments between life and death, where the soul lingers somewhere between the body and what comes after, Banza didn't think of any political affiliation. He was confused and wasn't sure where he was.

Was he in heaven or hell? Couldn't be hell since he felt no pain. But he wasn't in heaven either, because there were no angels around. He didn't feel as though he were falling or ascending. And where was his body? It must be somewhere. He was consciously thinking, but when he looked for his flesh and blood body it was nowhere to be found.

Then, from out of nowhere, he saw a sight that told him he was definitely dead but not dead like he thought dead would be.

He saw Naomi, his wife, with their little girl in her arms, and their son standing beside her. They were smiling as though welcoming him home to their traditional hut in his rural village. There was no soldier, nor any signs of their conflict. Banza was whole and had no marks on his body, or what he thought was his body. He was rested, hydrated, and felt like he'd eaten a four-course meal. Tremendous energy like he'd never experienced before, surged through his body.

With this new-found energy he yelled at his family, but when he opened his mouth, no words were heard.

Confusion washed over him. He heard his own voice but no one else heard it. What was happening? He couldn't hear his family and they couldn't hear him. Curse whoever was causing this to happen.

Furthermore, why torture him by showing his family alive and healthy. Weren't they all dead? How could he see them so vividly? Hadn't they been murdered when caught in a crossfire between soldiers and his comrades last year? Where they not buried at his home?

Naomi motioned for him to come to her, but as he sprinted, he was stopped by a force that prevented him from moving forward no matter how fast he ran. The sensation reminded him of a dream where he pumped his legs for all he was worth but remained in the same spot.

All of a sudden, they were gone. Darkness surrounded him as if he was in a large, empty auditorium. Metal scraping on metal caught his attention. He followed the sounds and found himself on a battlefield, but one like he'd never personally experienced. Two knights, clad in medieval armor, attacked each other with swords and shields.

Banza dodged from side to side. Were the knights after him? Safe on the sidelines, he studied the warriors. One was dark and the other white. But their differences were more than color. A stench like decaying flesh surrounded the dark combatant, while purity seemed to flow from the white knight's robe. The contrast was stark.

Why the disparity? The question lay heavy on Banza's heart.

Each time the knights' swords clashed, sparks flew. They fought on and on, but neither surrendered, nor did either appear to be tired. Who was winning? It seemed like a stalemate.

Then Banza could see beneath him as though he were hovering over his body in the African bush where he had just fought and died. It appeared he was elevated to some height, standing on a sheet of glass. What was that? Hyenas were already feasting on his body. By dawn, he would fill their bellies, and then a few days later, return to the earth from which he came.

Before he could bemoan his doomed corpse, the whole scene vanished, and Naomi appeared again, except this time without his children. She stood on mountain peak, and beckoned him to join her. But try as he might, he could not ascend to the place where she stood. There was a transparent barrier that prevented him from moving any farther. Cursing in every language he knew, gave him no relief. He was so close he could smell her hair, and admire the curvature of her pure form, but not taste her sweet lips.

Ever since his family died, he ached for them. He missed playing with his son, and nurturing his baby girl. And the nights. Oh, how lonely the nights were sleeping by himself. He missed making love with Naomi, and falling asleep beside her, and then waking up with his face next to her full, round, bare breasts.

Caught in this dream or perhaps not a dream but a vision or a different form of reality, he heard a voice. He knew God was speaking.

> "My frame was not hidden from you when I was made in the secret place. When I was woven together in the depths of the earth, your eyes saw my unformed body. All the days ordained for me were written in your book before one of them came to be."
>
> PS 139:15–16

3

The Terrorist's Conversation with God

The figure of Banza's mother appeared in front of him. Esther was his father's second wife.

How could this be? She'd been dead for years.

Esther had been bitten by a rabid dog, but his father ignored the encounter. However, once the wound became infected and Esther grew sick, he took her to the local bush clinic. But by the time the doctor examined her, the poison from the dog's bite had spread. The doctor told his father that it was best to leave Esther at the clinic so he could assure her death was painless.

As a little boy, Banza didn't want to leave his mother at the clinic. She was his life and comfort. She knew how to sooth his hurts, both physical and emotional. How could he abandon her? His father practically had to bind him with ropes and haul him away. But, in her last few coherent moments, she told him to leave because she'd see him in the next life. Her Christian faith,

Nails from Bullets

demonstrated in her life and love while he was a young boy, influenced him the most.

However, here she stood before him, not as his mother, but as God. He recognized her outward features, but instinct told him this was not really her. God resided in her body.

Esther reached out to him. He jumped back. Confusion and fear invaded his soul. He didn't want his mother, or God, to touch him until he had an explanation for this vision.

Instead, the soothing, loving voice of his mother surrounded him. "Don't be afraid son, I am your mother."

Banza gathered his courage and said, "I know you look like my mother, but my heart tells me you are God."

"You're right. I am God, but when my children come to heaven, they become part of me. As my word teaches, I am one with my children. What better way for heaven to greet you than to see your mother in God."

He shook his head in disbelief, and opened his mouth, but no words came forth.

She smiled. "I am here to answer your questions."

"How long have I been here?"

"Time, as you knew it, does not apply. Here we have no time. A few moments, or a thousand years, it's all the same."

"I don't understand." Banza scratched his head.

"Right now I don't expect you to. Take my word for it. Your circumstance here will soon make sense."

Esther paused. It was as if God in his mother waited for Banza to break down and drop his guard.

The urge to lower his barrier surged within him. He wanted to run into his mother's arms like he did when he was a scared little boy. His heart told him it was safe. Go ahead run and embrace the woman before you. So he finally did.

Arms wide, Esther rushed toward her son. They wept until tears streamed down their faces. Years had passed since they'd held each other. They could not hold each other tight enough.

"My son, my son, you have been lost, but now I have found you."

The Terrorist's Conversation with God

At her words, a chorus of a million angles began singing. "Hallelujah! Hallelujah! Praise God in the highest for one of his children has come home!"

Banza marveled at the magnitude of the chorus and the beauty of their voices. But a nagging question troubled him. "Where is my family?"

Releasing him, she asked, "Do you remember the cross on a chain Naomi was wearing when she was killed?"

"Murdered, not killed!" Deep anger tinged Banza's words. "Oh, I'm sorry Mother, I didn't mean to disrespect you. I have been angry for so long and I can't let it go."

"That's all right, son." Esther's voice softened. "I've been with you all your life and understand how you feel."

She took a step backward. "Did you ever wonder why Naomi was so happy after she started wearing the necklace?"

"No, I didn't have to. I knew she'd become a Christian."

"I know the manner in which your family was murdered enrages you. Believe me, not only as your mother, but as God, I hurt when you hurt. I ache anytime one of my children is in pain. I also know you lost your faith in me."

Thrusting his index finger at Esther, Banza yelled, "I stopped believing in you the day I buried my family. Are you trying to convince me you exist? You're wasting your time!"

"And yet here you are and here I am. Care to explain these surroundings some other way?"

A moment went by, or perhaps five thousand years before Banza responded. "Okay. You *do* exist!" He turned his back on her, then pivoted. "Then why am I here? Why haven't you sent me to hell where I belong?"

"I don't want to."

Not what he expected. "What do you mean you don't want to?"

"Do you see those two knights fighting over there?" Esther pointed to the arena.

"Of course I do. They've been fighting ever since I arrived here—wherever here is."

"No son, you're mistaken." Compassion coated Esther's words. "They began their battle the moment I conceived of you as a thought and your soul was born in my mind."

"That's crazy! Why should they care about me?" Banza's puffed out his chest. He would not capitulate. But the defenses he'd erected against his old faith began to dissipate, like embers from a fire falling to the ground and burning up from lack of fuel.

"They're fighting for your eternal destiny." Esther tilted her head, a sweet smile on her face. "The dark knight wants to take you to his master in hell, while the white knight's strong desire is to guide you to heaven."

After a pause, she asked, "Do you remember all those conversations you and your wife had late into the night?"

"Yes."

"Do you remember all the years I taught you about Jesus?"

Banza nodded as he lowered his emotional guard. His body relaxed, his shoulders sagged, arms loose at his sides.

"Your sweet wife and I were trying to save your soul." Esther's gaze searched his face.

He shoved his hands on his hips and looked away, afraid her piercing eyes would reach his soul. "I know. I know. But I don't need saving by you or anyone else." Banza's words were an automatic response. Is that what he really believed? He wasn't as sure about his position on God now as he'd been previously. Would he admit it? No way.

"Naomi and I were aware of the injustices you endured throughout your life." Esther seemed to pay no heed to his posturing. "Beneath all that anger and hate is a good man. A man who wanted something in which to believe but thought he'd lost all hope."

"But I did find a cause. One day we will run all the whites out of this country and take it back." Did he still believe the slogans he'd been taught by his communist benefactors?

"At what price?" Esther asked. "Have you not murdered, raped, and pillaged?

Chin jutting forward, Banza yelled, "All my deeds were necessary."

"So burning your own black people alive in their huts, or decapitating and impaling them, and murdering children and babies by cutting off their genitals and arms and legs make your actions right?"

Banza hung his head. Did he have any sensible reasons to justify his actions? No. With a mammoth sigh, he dropped to his knees and then laid flat on the clear surface. He howled like a she-wolf who'd lost her litter. Tears of repentance flowed from his eyes, forming rivers of crystal. Finally, the knowledge of where he stood and with whom he spoke penetrated the hard shell of disillusionment he'd constructed. All the justifications he'd manufactured for his lifestyle melted into the river. Although he was confused as to the nature of his enemy, he still wanted revenge.

Conversing with God! He couldn't deny it. He was dead and he saw the hyenas eating his earthly body. So what was he now? Spirit? Soul? A ghost? A demon?

His tears continued to flow, but Esther did not intervene.

Many minutes or centuries later, Banza asked, "Why save me? You know the kind of life I've lived. I don't understand."

"Man looks on the outside, but I examine the heart."

"I've done so many horrible things."

Esther drew in a deep breath. "Over two thousand years ago, there was a thief on a cross. He was just like you. He'd led an unholy life, but he, too, came to his senses just moments before his death, and asked for forgiveness."

"What happened to him?" Banza swiped the moisture from his face, and stood.

"My Son was on a cross next to him, and He said at that precise moment, the thief would be with Him in paradise. That man has been with my son ever since. The same reward awaits you."

"But I'm dead. The hyenas have already eaten my body. Isn't it too late?"

"I am *the* I Am, and I can choose to do what I want. Therefore, if I choose for you to have this last chance to repent and come to heaven, then that is my prerogative."

Esther's words softened Banza's heart to the point where his soul became receptive to God. But then he fisted his hands and glared at his mother.

Before he could utter a word, she said, "I can see you have a question. Is it possible for you *and* the man who killed you to be forgiven?'

"Would you save him after all *he* has done?"

"Only if he has a heart like yours."

Every muscle in Banza's body tensed as anger-heated blood surged through them. Esther's reasoning wasn't fair. The soldier deserved to die and go straight to hell. Banza was angry because his killer wasn't in torment where he belonged.

Banza gritted his teeth. Who was he hurting by clinging to his intense anger? No one but himself.

In spite of this realization, his hatred for the whites reignited and burn anew.

"Young man, you have a choice. Either you let the goodness I see in your heart grow so that you can accept my offer, or you can let your hatred take over your soul. If that's your choice, then you will lose our soul." Esther's voice held no emotion. "Some of my children have been rebellious up until the very end, even knowing the eternal consequences."

"Who for example?" Arms folded, Banza stepped closer to Esther.

"The second thief on the other cross. He had the same opportunity as the other man who humbled himself before my Son and asked for eternal forgiveness."

About this time, Banza's attention swiveled to the arena behind him where the battle continued. The dark knight appeared to be winning the contest. He beat his white opponent to the ground. The fallen knight desperately tried to hold onto his sword while fending off vicious strikes. His shield took several costly blows that also almost knocked it out of his other hand.

The Terrorist's Conversation with God

The scene took on a special meaning to Banza as he pondered his eternal choices.

Esther interrupted him. "You thought you lost your fight tonight when you were killed, didn't you?"

"Yes. I'm dead aren't I?" Sarcasm dripped off his words.

"You didn't lose. You won the fight with the soldier."

"What do you mean?" He shook his head. Had his mother gone mad? "How can you say that?"

"You won, because in losing the fight on earth, you can gain your soul."

He narrowed his eyes. "You caused me to lose my fight and end my life?"

"No. That's not what I mean. Before their creation, I know the length of the lives of each of my children, and the choices they will make."

Esther's words made no sense. Banza paced. "Then you determine their choices. And we are nothing more than puppets."

"No. Just because I know what you will do, doesn't mean I influence your decisions. You still have freedom of choice. I know the choices you have and their outcomes, regardless of what you decide. In your death, you have the chance to find life. But it's still your choice." Esther spread her arms wide. "So what have you decided?"

How could he answer her right away? He needed more information. "What are you going to do to with that soldier?"

"Son, don't worry about him. His destiny is between him and me. You have no say in what happens to him." She crossed her hands over her heart. "I love you and don't want you to lose your soul. The choice is up to you. So again I ask, what have you decided?"

At that moment the dark knight dropped his sword and shield, and disappeared in a cloud of dust. The hounds of hell howled. Faster and faster, his ashes swirled in a circle which was sucked into Death and Hades.

> "For none of us lives to himself alone and none of us dies to himself alone. If we live, we live to the Lord, if we die, we die to the Lord. So whether we live or we die, we belong to the Lord."
>
> ROM 14:7-8

4

The Medic

Tick bite fever.

Steve, a medic in the Rhodesian army, shrugged. How could he have been so stupid as to run out of medication?

Oh, my head hurts.

He'd taken the last dose of tetracycline, so now came the waiting game.

So many of the men had come down with the fever over the last few days that there was only one does left, which he used for himself.

Hope no one else contracts tick bite fever.

His unit was so far from civilization of any significance he didn't know how long it would take to get resupplied.

As shorthanded as they were, no one would be relieved of duty, even if the daytime temperature reached one hundred, or more. No one would be airlifted or driven out by vehicle, unless they had a life-threatening situation.

The Medic

Will have to be tough.

In reality, Steve was a medic in an army no bigger than a mosquito. That is, if you compared it to other armies in the world. Revolution was ripe in several countries all over southcentral Africa. Angola, Rhodesia, Mozambique, just to pick a few. That part of Africa was a mercenary's wet dream.

Steve was in the middle of this God forsaken country in the height of summer, whereas on the other side of the world where he was born, people were celebrating winter sports. He missed the four seasons. Here there was only one—hot, hotter, and hottest. Fighting is all he knew since he joined the American Army and served his time in Vietnam. After discharge, he tried to settle down in civilian life, but couldn't adjust. When he heard about friends in the same predicament, he joined them as a mercenary. Now two were dead, and he hadn't heard from or seen the others for over a year.

There's no comfortable place to rest. No matter how I sit or lie down. Feels like someone has my head in a vise grip, and slowly but methodically turns the screws tighter and tighter.

My body aches all over. Every joint feels like I'm being drawn and quartered. It's too hot to sit in my tent. Better to go outside somewhere.

But where?

Slowly Steve rose to a sitting position, with his legs over the edge of the cot. But each movement was a major effort in self-discipline, mind over matter. The intense pain reminded him of his first few days of basic training.

Hot air suffocated him. He had to get out of the tent.

I'd love to be in a nice pool, a glass of iced tea in hand with my baby by my side. That's if she hasn't dropped me and found some other guy. Probably has. Haven't heard from her in months.

Abandoning his comrades, Steve hobbled the length of the runway on his company's side of the airstrip. The army of a foreign country occupied the other side. Officially, they were not helping the Rhodesian forces in the terrorist war, and were prohibited from fraternization.

Nails from Bullets

They have better equipment and supplies than we do. Maybe when my gig is up I should enquire about how to join their army.

An empty chair in the meager shade of a scrawny thorn tree beckoned. A large communications radio sat abandoned near the chair.

No one around. No on-going missions.

Steve settled his aching body and squirmed until he was as comfortable as anyone could get in a canvas and steel-framed chair. He surveyed the area at the end of the packed dirt runway and sighed. Other than not being able to bathe daily, at least he had three meals a day, and he was not out on patrol.

A week after he finished his medic's course, he learned that one of the best students in his class was killed in an ambush. *Just goes to show, when your time is up, it's up.*

Steve closed his eyes. Hadn't he learned a Bible passage in Sunday School that refereed to man's allotted time on earth? What was the verse? He couldn't recall.

God looked down from his throne in heaven and saw Steve. God knew it was a matter of time before the two of them would be talking face to face.

A small group of terrorists had been surveying the airstrip for several days to learn its strengths and weaknesses. A few of them had walked all over the strip in plain sight. They knew the government soldiers could not tell them apart from the local bush Africans.

Tension had free reign in the band of terrorists. Like most groups, theirs included a hothead. The man didn't want to wait and attack at dusk, which would give them the night to get away. If the team had attacked when he chose, they would have all been killed. Phineas, their commander, had his hands full trying to keep him in line.

Just the other night there was a great opportunity to shoot down a plane that was about to take off. Phineas learned a few days later that one of the African soldiers in the Rhodesian army had accidently shot himself in the foot, and required an airlift to Bulawayo, the second largest city in the country.

In the pitch-black night, the airplane powered up at one end of the dirt airstrip. The makeshift runway had no lights, therefore a large truck at the other end of the strip faced the plane with its head lights on. The truck parked a few yards from the tree line so the pilot would know how far he had left to pull up before hitting the trees.

The perfect ambush. The terrorist group could shoot the plane, killing the pilot and his passengers, and then disappear into the bush. Phineas knew many of the government troops were away on leave. The meager force left behind would be hard-pressed to chase after them in the bush. They could score a kill, and make a clean get away.

Phineas was about to give his men the command to fire, when all of a sudden, two government troop carriers arrived. And to make matters worse, Phineas recognized special trackers in the mix. Their presence spelt death. He gave his men the order to stand down. All but one obeyed. The trouble maker wanted to attack anyway. Phineas almost had to coldcock him with the butt of his AK 47 before he complied.

Similar situation today. The hothead saw the medic sitting alone and isolated, and wanted to shoot him. Phineas explained all they had to do was wait until there was some noise to cover the sound of the AK 47. But this time the rebellious man wouldn't give up. He pulled a knife and Phineas defended himself. In a matter of minutes, he ended the life of his comrade.

Death and Hades were ecstatic. They watched the fight, and knew one way or another, they would receive at least one soul today. They were hoping for two.

God observed from above. The second a knife ended the life of the hothead terrorist, a deep pain seared God's heart. He was hoping right up until the last second that either one, or both, would repent of their dreadful lives.

Phineas commanded two of his men to pull the dead terrorist back into the bush. They found a safe place to bury him, and then covered their tracks. As quickly as they had appeared, they seemed to vanish. It was as though they had never existed as they melted into the thick bush. The rest of the group were glad their agitator was dead. They felt it would have been a question of time before his impetuosity brought death to them all.

God hates sin, and he despises sin even more when it consumes the souls of his children. He mourned the death of the terrorist. As the man's soul passed into Death and Hades, the celebration of hell at his coming poured forth like a carnival from Dante's Inferno.

Just like God would leave his ninety-and-nine to save one lost soul, so too will Satan rejoice to claim one dark soul. The terrorist's soul had been on the chopping block most of his life. Satan viewed his murder by his commander as great fortune.

God desires for his children to serve his purpose because they love him as a father. His heart breaks when they choose to follow Satan instead.

Dark clouds gathered from nowhere. Although out of season, rain fell over the terrorist's grave. The shower lasted a few moments.

> "Man's days are determined; you have decreed the number of his months and have set limits he cannot exceed."
>
> JOB 14:5

5

The Red Helicopter

In his sickness-induced stupor, Steve wasn't sure if he imagined events or not. Someone was watching him. He scanned the bush to his right and to his left. Nothing suspicious. He must be paranoid.

He continued his surveillance of the airstrip and supporting complex. Snorting, he summed up the situation in his mind. Not only was he in a God-forsaken country with an army the size of a mosquito, but the land was so remote, no one would take the time to swat the mosquito if it bit someone. Most of his family were ignorant of the name of the country. They thought it was in South America in spite of Steve telling them over and over it was southcentral Africa. Besides, didn't they know he couldn't speak a word of Spanish? He was in a country that spoke English—the King's English, as the locals liked to say. He didn't speak a word of the African language, and didn't need to learn because many of the black people spoke English.

Rested and less achy, Steve focused on the activity on the other side of the airstrip. A soldier was washing inside one of their helicopters.

Nails from Bullets

Interesting.

But wait. "What's that coming out of the helicopter?"

Not plain water. Blood from inside the medivac chopper turned the water a reddish color. Maybe wounded men had recently been retrieved from the battle zone.

All of a sudden a shrill alarm broke the silence of the bush. Terrorists have been spotted. The first-response chopper near Steve revved its engines. The huge propellers slowly rotated, which reminded him of a locomotive's wheels. It took a great deal of energy to turn them, but once in motion, nothing could stop them.

A bunch of young men scurried to the chopper and jumped in like they had done this hundreds of times before. Each sat with his legs dangling out the door. The chopper rose like a gigantic elephant. No matter how many times he'd witnessed the feat, Steve still could not believe it. How could something so large and bulky lift off the ground so gracefully? He was reminded of the Walt Disney cartoon where hippos preformed a ballet with art and grace while wearing little tutus.

Close enough to see the face of each soldier, Steve made note that they were all boys. Some were barely able to show a beard. They were tough, though. Special Forces. Who knew how often they had been the first-responders? How many of them who flew away today would be here to see the sun rise tomorrow? Who would give his life for king and country today?

From out of nowhere, a Bible verse popped into Steve's head. *Show me, O Lord, my life's end and the number of my days; let me know how fleeting my life is. You have made my days a mere handbreadth; the span of my years is as nothing before you. Each man's life is but a breath.*

Where did that come from?

Steve returned his focus to the chopper across the field. The man appeared to have concluded his chore. He threw the hose on the ground and turned off the spigot.

The soldier's callousness pierced Steve's heart. How could the man wash blood out of the chopper as if he were washing mud off a car? His actions, plus watching young boys fly off to battle, made Steve reconsider his relationship with God.

Life is short. Life is cheap. As fast as it is created and lived, so too can it be taken away.

Nope. He wasn't going to observe international protocol. He was going to cross the airstrip and walk right up to that soldier. Furthermore, he was going to learn whose blood was washed out of the helicopter.

Momentarily he forgot about his illness—how much every joint in his body ached, and how his head felt it was about to explode. He stepped onto the packed earth and endured the punishing heat from the unrelenting sun while he crossed the airstrip.

In less than two minutes, he stood in front of the red chopper. Yep, that's what he'd call it, the Red Chopper.

Steve introduced himself to the soldier, a young mechanic named Eric, and interviewed him. He learned that one wounded man was brought back from the bush. During an ambush, the guy had been hit in the right thigh, the bullets smashed his femur. His blood spayed everywhere inside the chopper. Eric added that after the Red Chopper landed safely, the pilot had a melt-down. Steve remembered reading about U. S. Marines during the Pacific conflict of World War II naming the phenomenon, "Going Asiatic". Combat-exhausted Marines who couldn't handle the battle stress would exhibit the thousand-mile stare, and be sent to a psych hospital.

But Eric added something different and unusual. "The medic on the chopper said this wounded guy was bleeding all over the place, obviously delirious, but he kept repeating a phrase."

"What did he say?" Steve asked.

"It was the most unusual thing he's heard, and he said he's been around lots of delirious men."

Impatiently, Steve asked again, "Well, what did he say?"

Eric hesitated. "You're going to think the medic is crazy." He paused and stirred up dirt with the toe of his boot. "The guy muttered, 'nails from bullets.'"

"What?"

"I said, nails from bullets."

"That doesn't make sense."

"You telling me? I have no idea what that means, and I've been thinking about it for the last two days."

"Spooky," Steve said. "What do nails from bullets have to do with him being shot all to pieces? In fact, what does it have to do with anything?"

Eric shrugged and lit a cigarette.

Meanwhile, Steve shoved his hands into his pockets. "What about the pilot?"

"Tony? He's a nutcase."

"What do you mean?"

"He says he saw Jesus." Eric took a long draw, then stubbed out the cigarette.

"What?"

"You heard me, he says he saw Jesus."

"He must be nuts. Why do you think he said that?"

"I don't know. All I can tell you is the scuttlebutt I've heard. Tony told his commanding officer he needed a break. Was at the end of his rope, and didn't want to go on anymore missions. His C. O. promised if he flew this last mission, he'd get a thirty-day pass. Obviously Tony took the assignment, but the return trip was a nightmare." Eric lit another cigarette. "The wounded soldier in the back kept yelling nails from bullets while his blood sprayed everywhere. To top it all off, the chopper was fired upon by gooks on the ground. All of this apparently pushed Tony over the edge."

"Wow, man. Did you see him?"

"Yeah. When he landed he looked like a statue. He went into what you docs call a catatonic state. Eyes looking straight ahead, frozen in his seat, and mumbling something about Jesus helping him fly the helicopter. It was freaky. Man, it was bizarre."

"Where's he now?"

"In our field hospital. They don't have a psych ward, so they thought he could use some rest until they can transport him to the city."

The wheels churned in Steve's mind. "Appreciate you talking to me. Do you think I could visit Tony and the wounded guy? What's his name?"

"Richard is the guy who got all shot up. Without a pass you'd have a hard time getting into the hospital because you're not part of our army."

"Okay. Thanks a lot. Better get back to my side of the strip."

"And I have a troop carrier to fix. See you around." Eric ground his cigarettes stub into the dirt and walked away.

Steve crossed the airstrip and returned to his chair in the shade. The recent conversation played over and over in his mind. Two wounded men, one physically, one mentally, with interesting experiences. Why had they chosen those specific words? Nails from bullets. Jesus helped me fly. He had to follow up on these two stories, but how could he safely enter the other army's hospital without being arrested?

Rubbing his chin, Steve evaluated various possibilities. He could lie, or appeal to everyone's sympathy. Why not just walk into the hospital as though he belonged there? After all, he was a medic. Clearly his uniform would shout that he did not belong in their military, but the colors on his belt indicated he was in the medical field. Maybe the staff at the hospital would recognize his right to be there. If anyone asked, he could say he was on a training mission under field operations. Made perfectly good sense to him.

"Okay. I'll do it."

After stomping across the strip, he easily found the hospital tent. Many beds were occupied by wounded men. He decided to visit Richard first, and asked a nurse for his location. She pointed to the end of a row, where the patient lay, his leg in a cast propped up by pillows.

"Good morning. My name's Steve Brooks. I'm a sergeant in the Rhodesian Medical Corps. Do you mind if I talk to you a bit?"

Richard grimaced. "Suppose not. I've got no big plans at the moment."

"I know you're tired and are recovering from a major wound so I won't stay long."

"Suit yourself." Richard squirmed in the bed, then sighed.

Steve almost left, but he had to take advantage of his subterfuge and assuage his curiosity. He got straight to the point. "You know how quickly word spreads. There's talk about your ride in the medivac chopper. Seems it was different than most."

"What do you mean?"

"They said you kept repeating a phrase all the way back."

Turning his head, Richard mumbled, "I don't want to talk about it."

"Why?"

"Because you'll think I'm crazy. Then you'll report what I say, and I'll be sent straight to the psych ward and labeled insane." The wounded man folded his arms. "What's that going to do for my record? I'll get an early discharge, and it will be the end of my military career."

"No, I won't. I'm here to help." Steve briefly touched the soldier's hand. "Besides, I'm bound by my oath. Unless you are suicidal or homicidal, I can't reveal anything you tell me."

A smirk covered Richard's face. "Yeah? The last time I trusted those words, as soon as I walked out of the counselor's office he was on the phone to my C. O. I learned never to have faith in you guys again. Medic, chaplain, or psychiatrist."

"I know. I know." After unfolding a metal chair, Steve sat close to the bed. "I encounter that fear all the time. Would it help if I told you I'm a Christian? Sometimes I think not a very good one and I am ashamed of some of the things I've done." Head lowered, shame heated his neck.

The soldier lay in silence for a few seconds. "Really? So am I. I feel the same way you do. There are no excuses for what I've done."

Excitement and another emotion Steve couldn't name surged through his chest. "Look, I don't claim to be a doctor, but perhaps a physician is not what you need. Maybe you need a fellow Christian."

Richard exhaled a long breath and seemed to relax. Then he asked, "I'm exhausted. Would you mind coming back tomorrow? Perhaps we can get an early start after breakfast."

"Okay. Unless I'm called out into the field, I'll be here at 0900 hours."

"Unless I (Thomas) see the nail marks in his hands and put my finger where the nails were . . . I will not believe it. Then he (Jesus) said to Thomas, 'Put your finger here; see my hands. Stop doubting and believe.' Thomas said to him, 'My Lord and my God!' Then Jesus told him, 'Because you have seen me, you have believed, blessed are those who have not seen and yet have believed.'"

JOHN 20:25-29

"He himself bore our sins in his body on the tree, that we might die to sin and live to righteousness. By his wounds you have been healed."

I PET 2:24

6

Nails from Bullets

Steve was not a morning person. Still groggy with sleep, he dragged himself out of bed. The sun's rays shed a golden glow through the tent. He blinked and rubbed his eyes, and then stuck his head out of the flap. Aah. Sunrise. Nothing could beat sunrise in the African bush. He'd been told that the dust in the air produced a series of colors that weren't duplicated anywhere else on earth. Skeptical at first, he was now convinced.

Nails from Bullets

Hands on his hips, he surveyed the span of vegetation in front of him, and drew in a deep breath. The sense of being in touch with nature, the earth, the soil, and God's creatures was profound. Poor slobs in the cities. Didn't know what they were missing.

At 0730 hours, the warmth of the sun felt good. Once the sun rose above the tree line, the heat would be intense. The freezing night temperature suddenly shot up like a tobacco sprout emerging from its soil bed.

Steve checked his watch. Too late for breakfast in the mess, but he didn't care. Powered eggs and fake ham with bread as hard as a rock weren't for him. He'd pick something up later on. Time to shower. Some shower. It was nothing more than a hose from a large tank of water tied to a tree branch. The ice-cold water took his breath away as he showered and shaved in record time. Then he ran back to his tent to finish drying off before he caught pneumonia.

While dressing, he gave himself a pep talk. "Steve, ol' chap. Walk across that airstrip and into their hospital as if you own it. Approach Richard as his doctor. Face any nurse with authority. Look her square in the eyes and stare her down so you won't have to talk."

He nodded once, and strode across the airstrip, 0900 hours on the dot.

No one hindered Steve's movements as he entered the hospital tent.

Richard turned toward him and raised his hand in greeting.

"Good morning," Steve said.

"Morning. I see you're a man of your word."

"How did you sleep?" Steve settled in the chair beside the bed.

"Not very well."

"Why? Were you in pain?"

Richard shook his head. "No. The meds help with that." He closed his eyes and whispered, "Certain events keep repeating in my mind. Almost like a vision or a dream."

Nails from Bullets

"Tell me about them." Steve had learned through experience that this phrase encouraged patients to open up about their problems.

"You said you're a Christian, right?"

"Yes, so, tell me what you experience." Steve knew he didn't want to dwell on his own guilt, and figured Richard felt the same.

But while he waited for the soldier to respond to his question, a flood of thoughts seeped through his mind. War and soldiering are not conducive to living a Christian life. A soldier has to perform so many un-Christ-like actions. Then there's the nature of killing that weighs heavily on the conscience.

And who could he talk to? Who would believe what any soldier had to say? If he's married, he won't talk to his wife. If he's single, he won't discuss his feelings with his parents or siblings. If he did open up, no one would be able to grasp the horrors.

Heroes? No soldier is a hero. He's only trying to survive. In war, it's the enemy or me. That simple. Either I live and go home at war's end, or my enemy does. I'd much rather it be me.

Steve was jolted back to the present when Richard spoke.

"I'll describe my vison, or whatever it is, but you're going to think I'm crazy."

Shaking off his dark thoughts, Steve said, "Hey, you can't be any crazier than I am."

"You've got to understand that of the six guys I started with three years ago, I'm the only one left." He swiped away a tear and turned his head.

Steve pretended not to notice. "Go on."

"I was there when each one of them died." This time, he couldn't hold back the tears.

Nothing Steve could say would ease the guy's pain. Steve let him cry. "Let it all out. I can sit here all day if you need." He handed the soldier a wash cloth he found on the next bed.

The minutes crept by.

Finally, Richard wiped his face. "First, there was John. Then Donald. Next, William and Harry both got it in the same op. And finally, Jimmy. Oh, Jimmy. Everyone thought that if anyone would outlive our group it would be him."

Richard broke down again.

Without thinking, Steve reached over and stroked Richard's head. Then he grabbed his hand and held it like his father would have done.

Through the sobs, the soldier continued. "I'm telling you, I shouldn't have gone on this op. I'm empty. I've nothing left. I told my C. O. but he said just one more." He pulled his hand free and covered his face. "I can't live with this guilt. What am I going to tell Donald's wife? What do I say to Jimmy's fiancé? How do I tell William's little boy? Every time they ask how each one of my brothers died, I have to lie." Sobs wracked his body.

Steve slumped in the chair. He had no words of comfort.

"I'm alive and they're dead. I'm alive and they're dead" Richard's voice trailed off into bitter weeping as he repeated the phrase several more times.

All Steve could do was rub the soldier's shoulder. He'd heard similar stories so often. But no matter how many times, he still didn't know what to say or do. After years of service, he concluded that he could do nothing except listen.

Time ticked by slowly.

Richard drew in a ragged breath. "Why am I alive and they're all dead?"

"I don't know." Steve shook his head. "I don't have any answers."

"You're a doc, you're supposed to know." Anger shot out of the soldier's eyes.

It didn't matter how many times Steve told the men he wasn't a doctor, they insisted on the word. He allowed Richard's accusation to settle, then he straightened his shoulders.

"That's what everyone thinks, but the truth is, even an experienced psychiatrist cannot answer your question. All he can do is give you a diagnosis, suggest therapy, or prescribe medication. The rest is up to you." Steve studied Richard's face to gauge the effect of his words. The man frowned, but appeared to be listening.

"Somehow you have to make peace with it. As a Christian, there're some things that happen in war, and life in general, that only God can judge."

"But it's not fair. Out of my group of pals, I'm the only one who has no wife, sweetheart, or fiancée." Richard's words exhibited a childish tone.

"Again, I have no answer, except that being fair has nothing to do with it. Life's not fair, never has been, never will be, until Jesus returns."

"But why did God allow my buddies to die?" A pout marred the soldier's face.

"I don't know. All I can do is offer my conclusion."

Folding his arms again, Richard said, "Let me hear it."

Steve eyed his companion. Yes, he was ready to *hear*. "In the beginning, God gave man and woman a perfect garden. He never intended for us, as their descendants, to experience war, pain, hunger, or hurt of any kind. Adam and Eve brought sin into the world when they disobeyed God. In caving to temptation and succumbing to their pride and vanity, they allowed Satan to usher in pain and death. And it will be that way until Christ returns."

Although Richard had his eyes closed, Steve could tell he was paying attention.

He concluded his thoughts. "So you see, God never intended for us, as his creation, to experience war. In fact, you might say the first war was between Cain and Abel. Cain disobeyed God and was jealous, so he killed his brother."

Neither man spoke for a minute or two. But Steve had one more point. "How is our war any different from wars throughout history?"

Shrugging, the soldier said, "It's not."

"And the world won't change so long as man continues to live without God, just like Adam and Eve, and Cain and Abel."

Richard crossed his arms and stared into the distance.

"I brought my Bible." Steve drew the book from his pocket. "You want to hear some scriptures that provide a few answers?"

"Yeah, okay."

Nails from Bullets

Steve opened the Bible. "First, I'll read from Isaiah 55:6–7. 'Seek the Lord while he may be found; call on him while he is near. Let the wicked forsake his way and the evil man his thoughts. Let him turn to the Lord, and he will have mercy on him, and to our God, for he will freely pardon.'"

The patient nodded.

Steve continued, "In other words, man is going to mess up. But if he changes his heart and turns to God, he will be forgiven, no matter how badly he thinks he's sinned."

"I understand, but it doesn't make sense."

"The next two verses in the chapter address your concern. 'For my thoughts are not your thoughts, neither are your ways my ways, declared the Lord. As the heavens are higher than the earth, so are my ways higher that your ways, and my thoughts than your thoughts.'"

Richard rested against the pillows, a frown across his brow.

Steve figured the man was contemplating the meaning of the Scripture, and gave him time to think.

Meanwhile, a nurse interrupted to take Richard's blood pressure. "A little high. How's your pain level?"

The patient pursed his lips. "Okay for now."

"Good." She removed the cuff and hurried out the door.

Steve used the break to change his tactics. "I heard you were delirious on the chopper. Seems you kept repeating three words over and over, and the medic with you couldn't understand the phrase."

"Yeah, that's what they tell me. What I can recall is really messing with my mind."

"Tell me."

"Before I went on this last mission, I wanted to die. I felt so guilty because it's not fair I am alive and all my brothers are dead." Richard rubbed his chin. "But when I got shot and thought I was going to die, that was like a kick in the pants. I *don't* want to die. I still feel guilty, but I want to live."

"I understand, but what was the phrase you kept saying?"

The patient paused and hung his head. "You're going to think I'm insane. So you must keep this to yourself."

Nails from Bullets

"I will. I promise."

"You promise?"

Steve held up two figures by the side of his head. "Scouts honor. I promise."

A minute crawled by before Richard spoke again. "Jesus was talking to me."

"Really? What did he say?" Maybe the young guy *had* lost his marbles?

"Jesus repeated three words. Nails from bullets. He said it over and over. I asked him what he meant, but he didn't answer me. He kept repeating the three words." A small smile crept over his face. "Funny thing though, each time Jesus repeated the phrase, I seemed to grow calmer. And then he finally said, 'I gave my blood on the cross through the nails in my hands and feet so that you could live and feel no more guilt.'"

Steve's eyes widened. The guy sounded so sincere. "Did Jesus say anything else?"

"Well, I told him I didn't understand, so he explained in detail. I remember his words exactly. He said, 'Turn your bullets into my nails on the cross so that you can experience my grace. Are not your bullets made from the same substance as nails? Why not turn your instruments of death into instruments of life?'"

The soldier's words washed over Steve and filled his heart. His mouth gaped open, and then he snapped it shut. Was the guy for real? "I'm confused," he said.

"At first I was confused, too, but the more I thought about Jesus' statement, the more it did make sense. When I focused on his nails, the less I thought about my bullets. His nails are more important than my wounds. The more I focused on his blood, the less I thought about my blood loss. Nails from bullets. Get it? I still suffer from guilt, but each time I recall Christ's voice, his words comfort me."

Steve slumped in the chair and scratched his head. *Did Richard really talk to Jesus, or was it his subconscious trying to make sense out of war? Was he hallucinating?* He shrugged and said, "Carry on."

Nails from Bullets

"I fought this revelation at first, but, odd as it sounds, it brings me comfort, so I stopped fighting." He looked up briefly, then leveled his gaze at the medic. "You're going to think I'm insane, but since I've told you this much, I might as well continue."

"Go ahead."

"Jesus didn't appear with a beard, robe, and long hair."

Okay. I'll humor him. "What did he look like?"

Richard rubbed his forehead. "Jesus came in the person of my dead father. My dad died when I was a boy, so I didn't have much of a relationship with him. Growing up, I longed to have a dad like all the other boys. I joined the Cub Scouts and Boy Scouts just so I could be with other dads, but it wasn't the same because they didn't belong to me. It was like I got a taste, but never a full stomach."

"Like eating one bite of a burger, but not the whole thing."

"Exactly." The patient pointed a bony finger at Steve. "You want to know why Jesus appeared in the person of my father?"

"Sure." *What was he going to say next?*

"He appeared in the person of my father because he knew my father was who I needed most to comfort me. I realized my dad is with Jesus, and one day I will be with both of them." A tear rolled down Richard's cheek.

Steve narrowed his eyes and stared at the man in the bed. *Was he for real?*

Richard's tired voice broke through the medic's musing. "Our conversation today has helped me. I still feel guilty, and don't understand why I survived and my friends died. Funny thing, I'm not as angry as I was before I went on this op. I know I have more healing to do in my heart, but I feel I'm turning a spiritual corner." He rested his head against the pillow. "I don't think our meeting was an accident."

Nodding, Steve shoved the Bible back into his pocket.

"Whew. I'm tired. Would you mind if we call it a morning?"

"No not at all. Let's pray before I go." Steve bowed his head. "Father, God, I think I speak for Richard here when I say we don't understand what he shared, but we do know you are in control. Thank you for your love, grace, and mercy. In Jesus name. Amen."

> "For our struggle is not against flesh and blood, but against the rulers, against the authorities, against the powers of this dark world and against the spiritual forces of evil in the heavenly realms."
>
> EPH 6:10–12

7

Ascension

Steve rubbed the tight muscles in his neck. These deployment trips were not fun.

"Hey, Doc, how come they made you a sergeant?" Charlie, the driver asked.

"I don't know. Just lucky I guess."

"You been a Doc long?"

"Oh, about five years."

Charlie was doing his best to generate casual conversation while driving at two o'clock in the morning. He and Steve were part of a four vehicle convoy to drop off a small search-and-destroy group of soldiers in a Tribal Trust Land. When Steve first arrived in Rhodesia he was quick to learn that a TTL was similar to a Native American reservation in the USA.

They were riding in a vehicle called a Rhino, a modified troop transport, heavily armored, and as sturdy as its namesake.

Ascension

It wasn't just dark, it was pitch black. Charlie couldn't turn on the headlights due to the clandestine nature of the mission. Each driver had to do his best to follow the vehicle in front.

This was the third deployment Steve had been on in the last few weeks. Army Intel reported a group of gooks were roughing up the locals, forcing them to provide housing and food when the government troops weren't around.

What were the local tribal villagers to do? The government troops approached the remote rural villagers and tried to win support by appealing to hearts and minds. The terrorists' methods were barbaric. They would come into the same villages a few days later. Cut off peoples' noses, ears, lips, tongues, and genitals. Then, as if that wasn't enough incentive, they'd make a lasting impression by either burning a family alive in their hut, or by impaling them in front of the village. So who would the villagers support?

Steve accompanied each deployment in case the men were ambushed. He'd provide first aid to any wounded guys. Over the last several months, no deployment convoy had been ambushed, and he didn't expect an ambush on this one either. It didn't make sense to ambush an armed convoy. Why would the gooks shoot at someone who would shoot back? It was much easier to assault unarmed villagers. Besides, there were always young women to rape. He'd heard stories of terrorists raping victims as young as seven or eight years of age. Now Steve had become so callous to their sexual predilections he even had a name for them. Rape 'em and bag 'em.

Out of nowhere, a brilliant, dazzling white light engulfed Steve. He immediately lost consciousness. When he awoke, he was as deaf as a door knob. A gooey liquid dripped into his eyes. His blood. The explosion must have caused him to bang his head against the iron-plated internal armor of the Rhino he was riding in.

He ignored his pain and deafness, and checked his limbs and torso. Whew! Intact. Surprise. He couldn't say the same for Charlie. Both his arms and his legs were shattered. Steve guessed much, if not all, the blood on him was not his own. After checking for a pulse in the driver's neck, Steve pronounced the young guy dead. He grabbed his medic kit and climbed out of the vehicle.

Tracer rounds filled the sky as if he were at a Fourth of July celebration. Most of the men in his Rhino had scattered to both sides of the road. At least one young soldier hadn't—his decapitated body hung out of the truck.

Following his training, Steve ran away from the Rhino. His fellow troops had created an extended line, and were giving back as much fire as they were taking. He dropped into what seemed like a natural gully just off the road. To his left lay one of the soldiers covered in blood. Steve crawled closer to administer first aid. But his action was a big mistake. Explosions illuminated both terrorists and government soldiers alike, making them easy targets. A terrorist must have had his rifle focused on the wounded soldier.

Just as Steve reached his intended patient, the dirt around him splattered with bullets pinging and bouncing. To protect the soldier, Steve wriggled up to him, and wrapped his body around him trying to make a protective cocoon.

Each bullet which found its mark in the soft flesh of the Steve's torso made a sickening thud.

"But God shows his love for us in that while we were still sinners, Christ died for us."

ROM 5:8

8

Grace

Then, something unexpected happened. Steve's thoughts became spoken words.

"What's wrong with me?"

"I'm not in pain and feel quite good."

"Where am I?"

A fatherly voice answered, "You're in Paradise."

"Who said that? I didn't ask that question out loud. I only thought it."

The same voice he'd heard before floated to his ears. "It doesn't matter if you use words or thoughts here. We communicate either way. You'll get used to it."

"What do you mean, I'll get used to it?"

"Open your eyes." The fatherly voice held a note of tenderness.

"They are open."

"Open the eyes of your heart. You'll see so much more."

A vast panorama appeared before him. "Wait a minute. What am I lying on? I can see below as though I'm looking through a glass. I see my own body. How can that happen?"

"Your body was killed."

"You mean I'm in heaven?" Steve asked.

"No, not quite. It's Paradise. An in between spiritual existence until my Son returns to the earth again to establish his kingdom."

"So am I in between heaven and hell?"

"What do you think?" There was no criticism in the fatherly voice.

"It must be heaven. I don't feel any pain. In fact, I've never felt better in my life." Steve thumped his chest.

"Of course. Now look below you."

"Hey, wait a minute. I can see where I just came from. That's the site of the ambush."

"You're right."

"I see my body. Looks like I'm still coiled around the guy I was trying to protect."

"You are," the voice said.

"Looks like the firefight is over and our guys are checking the gooks' bodies to be sure they're dead."

"Right again."

"Hey. They're rolling me off that guy, and checking my pulse." The sight of someone lifting his wrist seemed surreal.

"Notice they are shaking their heads."

"Yeah, now they are checking the guy I was wrapped around. His pulse is good. They're calling a stretcher. Hey, I saved his life." Joy flooded through Steve.

"Feels good, doesn't it."

Steve nodded. "Great."

After the elation of witnessing the life and death scene, the reality of Steve's own death began to set in.

"I'm dead, aren't I?" He sat down and crossed his legs. The weight of his newfound state took its toll. Dead. Gone. Forever.

"Yes."

"I won't see my family, my home again. I won't see my dog. What will my mom and dad do when they learn of my death?"

The voice then offered words of comfort. "I know this is a big transition, and it will take a while to adjust, but death is part of life.

Grace

Death begins at birth. From the moment of your birth, each day draws you closer to the day you'll die. Your family will grieve, but over time, they will accept your fate."

Alone in the vast emptiness, the medic sat down. He was dead, in Paradise. The voice had overwhelmed him with information.

From a human point of view, time went by, but how much, no one knows. For in Paradise, an hour could be a day, or a day a thousand years.

Steve had been deep in thought and decided to ask God some questions. It didn't take a brain surgeon to understand the fatherly voice was God.

"God?" Steve asked.

"Yes, I'm here."

"I've been thinking."

"Indeed. About what?"

Steve hesitated a moment, or a year. "I don't deserve to be in heaven."

"Well, my son, no one deserves to be in heaven."

"Yes, but I'm different."

"How?" God asked.

"You don't know about the things I've done." Weighed down by guilt, Steve bowed his head.

"Do you mean the time you were tempted to let a terrorist die and no one would have been the wiser, because it could have been concluded he died from his wounds? Or the time you visited the bordello over and over because you thought you were in love with one of the girls? How about all the times you went to strip clubs, became drunk, used drugs. Remember when you slept with your fiancée's best friend at your engagement party?" God seemed to take a deep breath. "But I would say probably you feel the most guilt about the men you killed in battle, especially the ones you captured and then killed while prisoners. How about all the mornings you missed worship services, were angry at me, drove by church buildings and expressed crude hand gestures?"

"Okay, God, I get the picture. I forgot you were present from before we are born until the day we die." Steve shrugged. "But you made my case. You know all my sins, and yet you let me in heaven. Why?"

"Son, first of all you have to remember man looks on the outside, but I look at the heart. Yes, you committed many sins, but your heart was hurting. You were acting out of anger and not because your soul was toxic. In fact, if anything, your heart was pure."

"Wait a minute, God. How could my heart be pure?" Scratching his head, the medic frowned.

"Because your acts did not reflect the true you. Your heart was affected by all the orders you had to obey, although they went against your convictions, and not because your heart was filled with evil."

Steve's head dropped. He covered his face with his hands and wept. "I still don't deserve heaven. I don't deserve your forgiveness. I don't deserve your mercy or your grace."

"That's right, my son, you don't. What do you think grace means?" God paused a moment. "So let me make another point."

"Okay."

"If your heart was toxic or evil, would you be making a plea to revoke my pardon?" God asked.

"No, I guess not."

> "No one has greater love than the one who lays down his life for his friends."
>
> JOHN 15:13

9

The Choice

Time stood still as Steve took stock of his situation. Was he really having a conversation with God?

The Sovereign's voice interrupted. "Son, let me ask you some questions."

"Okay."

"Do you remember how you came to be here in Paradise?"

"Yeah, I died in that ambush."

"No, it was more than that."

"I don't understand." Confusion clouded Steve's mind.

"What did you do down there on earth?"

"I did my job."

"You did much more than your job."

"How so?" Perplexed, the medic tried to look into God's face, but His glory was too great to be witnessed by man.

"You didn't have to crawl up to that wounded soldier and protect him with your own body."

"But that was my job. It's what we're taught to do."

Nails from Bullets

"No, you could have stayed in that furrow in the ground, safe and sound, until the fight was over. But you chose to save that young man's life by giving your life. That was not your job. That was your choice."

> "And the devil, which deceived them, was thrown into the lake of burning sulfur, where the beast and the false prophet had been thrown. They will be tormented day and night for ever and ever . . . Then death and Hades were thrown into the lake of fire. The lake of fire is the second death. If anyone's name was not found written in the book of life, he was thrown into the lake of fire."
>
> REV 20:10, 14–15

10

Prelude

Steve accepted God's answer. However, he needed time to internalize the concept. He continued to believe he shouldn't be in Paradise. He knew far too many men who were better than he.

However, he did have one more question for God. "Excuse me, sir."

"Yes, my son"

"I noticed something unusual when I arrived. Even after my head cleared, it still doesn't make sense to me."

"What is it?" God asked.

"I saw two angelic knights fighting with swords and shields."

"Correct. So what's your question?"

Steve shoved his hands into his pockets. "Who are they and what are they fighting about?"

"The dark knight is an angel of Satan, and the white knight is my angel. They were fighting for your soul."

Not the answer he expected. "Really? How long have they been fighting?"

"They began fighting before we counted time. Since before your conception, and farther back to when the earth and all that's within it were just an idea in my mind."

Another millennium passed while Steve digested God's wisdom. Then he gathered the strength and courage to question God and pointed in the direction of the swordsmen. "Why defend my soul before my birth?" There seemed no end to the questions stirred up in Steve's mind.

"Let me explain. If you want to build a boat, you draw up the plans, gather your supplies and tools, and start building. Weeks later, you have a boat. When I created the Garden of Eden, I said the words, and it was. From the smallest insect to the planets of the universe, all came about at my word. So if these creations and the duration of their lives are set by me, would I not value more every human being? Is it not written in my word, that man was created in my image?"

"Whew. Do they ever quit?"

"Yes."

He had to know more. "When?"

"When someone makes a choice. Satan over me, or me over Satan."

Again with the choices. "How does that work?"

"The black knight is fighting for as many souls as he can collect. He thinks that if he kills the white knight, he will win the soul they are fighting over. He also believes that the more souls he can collect in conquest, the greater favor he can gain from his master, Satan. Trouble is, his master doesn't care about his demons. His only concern is the number of souls each can collect. He sweetens the pot by convincing his demons that the ones with the most souls will avoid being thrown into the place of eternal torment. They have forgotten one important fact—he is the Father of all lies."

Prelude

Steve nodded, although he didn't fully understand God's words. However, he didn't have long to wait for additional information.

"What these black demons of Satan don't understand is that they can't kill the white knight. They only collect the souls of humans who have already made their choice for Satan, made in the bodies of each human before their deaths. The soul who decides to follow me is ushered up to heaven by the white knight, which ends the fight. Sometimes souls like yours need a little coaching, then we keep them here until they make a decision."

"Then what happens to the dark knights when a soul decides to go to heaven?" Steve asked.

"They turn into a fine, black, foul-smelling dust which is wafted away by the odious breath of the Evil One. The voices of those in the pit, and the ones falling down into it, are so tortured in agony I have blocked you from hearing them. Satan keeps a written record in his own book of those who have chosen him, that is, until the second coming of my son, Jesus. In the meantime, doomed souls begging for mercy are like a symphony to his ears."

Steve surveyed his surroundings. "But where are these battles taking place? I only saw the one for me."

"To protect you, I have kept the full battlefield out of your vision. I am afraid if you witnessed the full scope of the eternal battle for human souls, the shock would be too much for your mortal eyes."

"After all I've seen and done, you think I can't handle it?" the medic asked.

"Your human ears and eyes can't endure the sounds of death on such a massive scale. The piercing of your heart by the voices of the lost would be too much for you to bear. Even the angels never go near such vile corruption, that is, except the ones fighting for souls. All the heavenly host have the freedom to view the full battlefield any time, but they don't, because they too don't wish to be anywhere near the carnage."

God's explanation intrigued Steve. "Please, I would like to see field."

"All right. Brace yourself because I will open the eyes of your heart, but only for a moment. You must cover your ears with your hands. Keep your mouth tightly closed, and take a deep breath and hold it. Do not breathe even for a second. Finally, sit down and bring your knees up to your face and bow your head, blocking your vision. Place yourself into as tight a ball as possible."

Puzzled, he hiked a shoulder. "But Lord, I'm spirit now, not human."

"I don't have time to explain. Just do what I say."

Reluctantly, Steve assumed the sitting position God instructed.

"One last word of warning," God said.

"What's that?"

"Are you familiar with the story when I told Lot and all his family to leave Sodom and Gomorrah?"

"Yes." Steve nodded his head against his knees.

"Do you remember what I told them *not* to do?"

"You said don't look back."

"What happened?"

Lifting his head, he rubbed his eyes. "When you destroyed the two cities, Lot's wife looked back."

"What happened to her?"

"She turned into a pillar of salt."

"Remember what happened to her when you are tempted to uncover your ears, or open your eyes, or take a breath."

"Will I turn into a pillar of salt, Lord?" Steve asked.

"Worse. Now follow my instructions."

Steve pulled his torso and limbs as tightly together as he could. He covered his ears, and bowed his head.

"Ready?"

"Yes."

Then God said, "Now."

In the time it takes a human to blink, God allowed Steve to see an eternity of conflict between the forces of good and evil. The medic was thankful his exposure was no longer than a second, and wished he had listened to God and not seen what his heart saw.

Prelude

"Oh my God. My Lord. My Master. I had no idea of the horror," he yelled.

"As a mortal, you wouldn't have known."

The experience so threatened Steve's sanity that he had to describe the scene. "I saw a dual world of what is paralleled by what could have been. The most evil person I have ever seen stood before me." Steve shook with fear. "He scared me so much, I cried like a little child. I wanted to run and find my daddy to protect me, because I was afraid this creature would consume me. He was surrounded by millions just like him."

"Could you identify him?"

Shaking his head vigorously, he mumbled, "No."

"It was *you*."

"Me?" He scrunched up his face in disbelief.

"Yes, you."

"I don't understand." He gulped. "How could it be me?"

"It was you, if you'd chosen to follow Satan."

A heaviness swarmed over Steve, but God wasn't finished yet.

"It wasn't just you by yourself, but the collective you. It was all of those who seek Satan. One by one, as he collects lost souls, they are thrown together to make them stronger and stronger. This gives them a collective voice to create a stronger lie. Their purpose is to be so strong and powerful that even the most resolute of souls who want to follow me, will join them instead. This collective of the lost is a persona of the Father of Deception."

God's words penetrated Steve's shell, but he didn't respond.

"That's why he's so powerful. Didn't you feel drawn to come out of your fetal position and join him?" God asked.

"Yes."

"Why?"

"I saw the most exquisite meadow surrounded by snow-capped mountains. A rippling stream cascaded into a peaceful lake. Beautiful birds fluttered above as sunset colored the sky. I saw—"

Nails from Bullets

God interrupted. "Satan, the father of lies made you see beauty in death and destruction. He presented the earth more beautiful and inviting than anything else you had ever seen."

"Yes, how did you know?" As soon as the words left his lips, Steve realized how foolish they were since God knew everything.

"Satan uses what he knows will appeal the most to draw souls away from me. To some, he promises money, to others, women or men. Some are offered their health, or recovery from a terminal disease. Other ploys he uses is to promise they can be with partners lost through old age and death. He offers power to rule, even eternal life. But on this last promise, he doesn't explain where this eternal life will be spent. He makes you believe I am offering eternal life in heaven."

Caught up in the drama of the moment, he said, "You know, God, it wasn't just that I saw beauty beyond what I could imagine, but I heard beauty as well."

"I know. Tell me what you heard."

This time the medic didn't ask how God knew he'd heard something spectacular. "I'll try to explain. It wasn't earthly music or singing, but an appeal to my ears in such harmony and sweetness of pitch that begged me to draw closer."

"And what else did you experience?" God asked.

"Even though I held my breath and kept my mouth closed, I could smell a fragrance somewhere between freshly baked bread from an old fashioned kitchen, to a grilled steak."

"What did this aroma make you desire?"

"The delicious smell attempted to lure me from my fetal position, but I remembered what you said." Steve pointed toward God's presence. "I had no idea the deceptive power of this war."

"How would you? This battle has been raging since before the creation of man, and has spread beyond what the human eye can see and endure. You didn't see thousands, or hundreds of thousands, but tens of millions of single battles. Each battle has a goal to use every deception possible to lure man away from me and toward Satan. The sacrifice in each battle is not in blood but in truth."

Prelude

"Oh, my Lord and God." Steve dropped to his knees. "Please show this suffering to mortal man. Then he will stop his wars, and he may even change his heart toward you."

"You know my son, I have spent eons thinking about your request, but I concluded if man saw what you witnessed he would not stop his wars nor make a choice for me."

"Why, my Lord and King?"

"Man has not learned from his own history, and because in his freedom to choose, his pride will always be manipulated by Satan. This carnage won't stop until the second coming of my Son. My children have had my word for over two thousand years, and it seems fewer and fewer read it, much less believe it."

> "So do not fear, for I am with you; do not be dismayed for I am your God. I will strengthen you and help you; I will uphold you with my righteous right hand."
>
> ISA 41:10

11

Copilot

Another span of time evaporated. Steve considered God's last words, and nodded. Yes, man never learned from his mistakes.

He tapped his chin and said, "My Lord and King, I do have one last request before you take me to heaven."

"What is it my son?"

"I never had a chance to talk to Tony, the pilot of that helicopter."

"Don't worry my son. You're not the only Christian concerned about him."

"Really?" Steve smiled. "Who else went to see him?"

"He was sent to another facility where a psychiatrist treated him."

"That's great. Is he okay now?" he asked.

"Yes."

"What happened?"

"A nurse where he was being treated is also a believer. She was fascinated by what she learned from his medical records where Tony indicated that he saw Jesus on his return trip."

"That must have gotten him a section eight." *Poor chap. Institutionalized.*

"No. The sympathetic doctor was willing to say that if Tony thought he saw Jesus, then it didn't matter how other people reacted. The doc was more concerned that the pilot was not claiming to *be* Jesus. Tony never claimed to be Jesus or God, or any other deity. He only claimed that Jesus helped him fly the helicopter on its return trip."

Steve said, "I guess that makes sense."

"The doctor concluded Tony needed Jesus to help him fly the helicopter because he alone couldn't do it anymore. The doctor didn't know that my Son was *in* the helicopter. He was helping both Tony and Richard during their ordeal. I am with all my children throughout all their lives, whether they accept me or not."

"I'm beginning to understand."

"My son, I need to tell you the rest of the story," God said.

"Okay, my Lord."

"Do you remember how Richard, the wounded soldier, told you he saw Jesus, how my son appeared in the form of his father?"

"Sure, I remember."

"Tony also needed to see and feel he was being helped by someone he loved and missed."

"Who did he see in Jesus?" By now, Steve accepted without question or doubt how God worked.

"He saw his mother."

"What did he need from her?"

"Tony's mother was killed in a car accident when he was ten years old. He was in the front seat when the accident happened. They both had their seat belts on, but the impact from the car that hit her door was so severe it killed her instantly. Like many children his age, he blamed himself for her death. He lived his whole life thinking he could have done something to save her. He had a good father, and brothers and sisters, but no matter what they did to help him understand it was an accident, nothing they said change his mind."

Steve's eyebrows rose. That made perfect sense.

"When my Son appeared to him as his mother, it was a shock at first, and he thought he was hallucinating. But during the flight, my Son, in the spiritual body of Tony's mother, not only helped him fly the helicopter, but that assistance helped lay his guilty conscience to rest. It was a peace he had been seeking all his life."

"That's beautiful."

"I write through the Apostle Paul in the book of Hebrews that many Christians have been courteous to strangers not knowing they were angels. There are some Christians to whom my Son appears when they need him, but he appears in the human form they need most."

Steve rubbed his chin while internalizing God's words. "Until now, I had no conception of the breadth and depth of your love. May I ask you another question?"

"Sure."

"Do you watch over the lives of unbelievers as well?"

"I am with all my children. I am like any father on earth. Does an earthly father stop being a father because his son rebels?"

"No." Steve glanced above trying to find the figure of God, but only light surrounded him. "But I don't understand how you could be equally close to unbelievers."

"Every child born has a mother and father, but they all belong to me. I stay by a child even when his parents abandon him. If parents decide to abort a baby, I'm with that child. In the case of a miscarriage, I'm there beside the baby. I am with the child given up for adoption. No matter the circumstances, I'm present through sickness, disease, addictions, divorce, criminal activity, and especially, war."

"Father, are you also with our enemy?" That question had burned deep in Steve's soul for many years.

"Before I answer, let me ask you a question. Is every child born on this earth *my* child?"

"Of course," Steve said.

"Then, am I with the enemy?"

"I don't understand how you can be." The medic turned around. Where was God? "The people we fight have committed terrible, inhumane atrocities."

"Remember what I just said. No parent abandons a child especially when that child is misbehaving. Not only am I beside the enemy, but with the convicted murder, the thief, the psychopathic killer, the rapist, and all of my children, no matter what they have done."

Steve reeled at God's words. "But how could you love them?"

"I want my children to know that I will never stop loving them no matter what evil actions they commit. They need to know that I won't accept their evil deeds or thoughts, but I will always love them. And they each need to know I will be with them right up until the end, even when they have chosen Satan over me. It hurts me to see my children in pain, whether they are obedient or disobedient. A very sad reality for some people is that on their deathbeds after all earthly beings have abandoned them, I will still be there. "

"I never thought of it that way."

"One last point I want you to understand," God said.

"What's that, Father?"

"I don't rejoice when any of my children enter the eternal pit. I receive no pleasure or sense of vindication by their eternal punishment. I know they made the choice independently, in spite of all my ovations to embrace me. They have free will, but I want them to *choose* to love me because that is the only way for them to be happy in heaven. What hurts me the most is not only will they have an eternity of pain in hell, but the fact they decided to reject me."

"But you are God." Steve frowned. "Why would you make yourself so vulnerable?"

"It's because I am God and have *chosen* to make myself vulnerable. Pure love has to be vulnerable or it's not love, but selfishness. Understand?"

"I think I'm beginning to."

"Okay, then, let me put it to you this way," God said. "Are the parents of a convicted murderer more saddened by the fact that their child is to be executed, or by knowing their child chose evil over good?"

"I never thought of it that way either."

"The parents are hurt because they have made themselves vulnerable. That is the only way to love purely. When this selfless love is not returned, it is the greatest pain any human can experience. As the father of all, I experience the same hurt."

> "And the great dragon was thrown down, the serpent of old who is called the devil and Satan, who deceives the whole world; he was thrown down to the earth, and his angels were thrown down with him."
>
> REV 12:9

12

Orientation to Death and Hades

Thousands upon thousands of recently perished new dark souls were free-falling through a gloomy, menacing, thick cloud. How thick, no one demon or mortal has known since the beginning of time. The cloud was the ceiling of Death and Hades, and there was no end to the raining of souls. They all seemed to be spewed out like missiles, as if someone hit a toothpaste tube real hard. Unlike an earthly storm where rain ranged from sprinkles to torrents, these dark souls, sometimes referred to as new recruits, poured steadily through the clouds, with no end in sight. This consistent rain of souls had significantly increased over the centuries.

It seemed that as man became more enamored with himself through science, the less he felt the need for God. Man believed he was god and master of his own fate. In this primitive stage of his evolution, man created a God to make himself feel secure in an unsafe world. Now that he was governor of his life, the earth, and the universe, he no longer needed a deity. Instead, he developed new gods he worshipped, such as wealth, power, and a deeper sense of his own narcissistic pride.

Satan's work of collecting souls simultaneously became easier as millennia passed. He no longer used primeval fear as he had done in earth's first few thousand years. Now all he had to do was take advantage of mankind's desire to follow his own natural hedonistic inclinations. Satan discovered from the Garden of Eden that temptation was easy, because most men did not know how to manage the power of free choice.

Men who had chosen to follow Satan died in the most gruesome ways—hideous consequences of a dark life uncontrolled in the flesh. Consequently, the Evil One exploited this failing for his advantage. Thousands of his adherents were murdered, died of social diseases, were involved in accidents that could have been avoided had they lived a Christian life. Many were murdered by poisoning, hangings, were butchered, or shot. These dastardly deeds were often perpetrated by the closest members of their families, by sons or daughters or wives who wanted an inheritance sooner than the natural death of the person could provide. Like those people who committed murder, these souls were also intoxicated by power and wealth, and would soon be in Satan's steady diet of tasty slimy stew.

Satan's appetizing delicacies were amply supplied by other classes of men. There was a steady flow of middle class and poor alike, who admired the wealthy and powerful for their status. These poor souls spent a lifetime in pursuit of a hopeless, hollow dream, and ended up no richer or wiser. They never learned that happiness was not found in what a person owned, but in what was given. So, in Death and Hades, they also became the buffet supreme for Satan and his chief captains of sin.

Rich and poor souls alike never appreciated God's freedom of choice and the importance of trust. There are two truths about this freedom Satan hoped many humans would never learn. So far, he had been successful in exploiting the greed and lust for power of many humans who selfishly misused the freedom of trust. This abusive demonic policy had kept a steadily increasing quantity of souls for Satan's meat locker.

The first truth is that man has to be given unconditional trust in order for him to be free to decide if he will honor this gift. The reason is simple; a person cannot fully honor what is not in his full possession. When God offers man the virtue of trust, he is offering him a spark of deity and a glimpse of eternity.

The second truth is that God's offer of trust to man entails an inherent risk—the possibility that man will break God's trust. However, God is willing to take this risk because he wants man to love him voluntarily, from his own heart. Anything less, dilutes the nature of trust.

The perfect storm of Death and Hades expanded as far as the eye could see, brimming with tempests, rain, tornados, and hurricanes. But it was the borders of Death and Hades that scared the novices of torment the most. As they fell, they could see through the partitions as though they were made from clear, thick plastic. Thousands of souls on the other side were seeking to escape their misery. They were dressed in clothing that indicated the time period from which they came, going back millennia in man's history. As the wretched souls tried to escape, they pushed their hands, faces, arms, legs, and feet against the border. The clear barrier fit like a glove around each extremity. Since the partition was pliable yet sturdy, it acted like a trampoline and flung the souls backward.

These souls weren't being physically tortured by demons with vats of oil and roasting fires, but by the false gods of their earthly existence. Satan also used their peculiar, private phobias to target their fears. Regardless of the personal fear each unsuspecting dark soul had hidden for a lifetime, each was known by Satan. What the dark souls failed to realize is their individual phobias had been catalogued by Satan and his clerical staff in their small spiral black books. This vital information was neatly and quietly recorded and held in perpetuity until each soul's death.

Nails from Bullets

Satan had the power to switch the souls from spiritual to human form in a blink of an eye. They had flesh and bones one minute, and were ethereal the next, whichever form he needed to enhance their pain and suffering.

Those that had power during the flesh were attacked by hundreds of beings they at one time represented. People these politicians had lied to and deceived by making promises of fairness and equity, were now all privy to their new bodies in Death and Hades. On earth, these deceptive politicians' constituents could only mumble and threaten, but in Death and Hades, they could bite, kick, punch, and hit with impunity. These officials were receiving a beating for eternity. Their punishment was compounded by the fact that no matter how they were abused, they could not escape, because they were already dead.

To Satan the beauty of this torment was not how badly these former powerbrokers were being beaten and could never die, but in how he'd fooled them. They each had a mere lifetime of being inebriated by power. They drove the best chariots or cars, or rode the best horses, lived in the finest homes, ate the richest food, and traveled at government expense. Their gods of affluence, were ironically, the source of their eternal punishment. They traded their years on earth for eternity in hell—Satan's best bargain.

The falling souls from the earth could also see a different type of torture earmarked for the rich and powerful who had followed no rules to obtain their wealth. This punishment was not metered out on people who became wealthy through hard work and sacrifice. Oh no. It was set aside for the wealthy who crushed others to get to the top.

Satan reserved a unique paradox for this group of souls. As they floated into Death and Hades, they'd been given numerous bags of gold and silver. The walls of their rooms were made of gold, with silver bars stacked as far as the eye. Each lost soul was ushered into a room filled with boxes of diamonds, rubies, and exotic jewels.

Upon arrival, the doomed soul was wild with ecstasy, and thought he was in heaven. He laughed, and became mad with delight as he rolled around his room reveling in his new financial affluence. His antics resembled a child playing in a toy store.

But then something odd began to happen. The room started filling with water. At first, the dark soul was intrigued, but as the water began to rise, he panicked. Where was the door? How about a window? But there was no means of escape. Eyes bugging, he realized the room would fill with water and he would drown. He struggled to kick his legs, but he quickly learned bags of gold and silver were permanently attached to his feet. A sad reality dawned—his feet were glued to the very commodity he worshipped

Water rose to his chest. He tugged and pulled at the bags to no avail. It was just a matter of time before he'd drown.

Here is where his fate made Satan's day. The soul was already dead so he couldn't drown, but this fact did not stop Satan from allowing him to drown to the point of asphyxiation, over and over for eternity. A similar fate awaited other doomed souls who in human form had been deathly afraid of water.

Those formally wealthy who were afraid of fire, were sent to rooms with the same gold and silver contents, except they were trapped inside, and would burn to death over and over. For those souls who were petrified of reptiles, Satan had rooms set aside, decorated as aforementioned, but also filled with pythons and alligators, so the damned would be eaten alive continuously for eternity.

The first rude awakening of the seriousness of Death and Hades occurred for each soul as they descended, regardless of whether they were punished immediately after entering their doom or not. If what they had seen through the partitions as they fell had not made them aware of their dark demise, then what happened when they hit the floor surely did. Although they had fallen a long distance, it only took a short amount of time. Or, if Satan could see they had a fear of heights, he would make their fall as long as possible until he became bored with their yells and screams. Either way, when they hit the floor, every bone in their bodies were broken. Faces were smashed beyond recognition, with some impacts so hard, eyes popped out of their sockets.

Nails from Bullets

In these souls' earthly lives, such falls would have killed their bodies. But since they were not capable of dying again nor elapsing into unconsciousness, they had to feel these disfigurements and brokenness in all their agonizingly glorious pain.

Satan and certain of his chief followers had the best ringside seats to watch doomed souls hit the floor of Death and Hades. The spectacle of souls writhing in pain and agony as broken bones pushed through flesh, and blood spewing out from hearts still pumping, elicited roars of laughter from the evil spectators. It reminded history of the Romans and their gladiatorial arenas.

Although spirit and no longer human, the lost souls resembled their mortal forms, and were composed of a substance known only in the spiritual world. These corporeal shapes were necessary in Death and Hades so that their suffering could be carried out in any way Satan wished to torment them. He could cause them to exist in a living hell spiritually, mentally, or physically. His special enjoyment was developing pain in all three states.

These initiates to eternal pain and suffering had no idea they were fresh meat to be devoured by the Dark Master himself, any time, any way he chose.

The condemned cannon fodder, reserved for the Evil One's pleasure, was ushered into different lines according to a color each had stamped on his forehead. Once Satan and his royal court had enough laughs at their fall, the master allowed them to immediately heal so they could proceed into special orientation rooms for their new eternal lives. The special colored stamps on their foreheads matched the color over the mantel of the doors.

Thousands of dark souls were arriving every minute. They filled the orientation rooms of Death and Hades as they were herded in like cattle. The commotion was deafening, similar to a crowd at a football arena trying to escape an out of control fire. The collection hall into which new arrivals from earth first gathered was so large none of them could see its front or back walls.

When the dark souls looked up they were surprised that they weren't underground—as humans had portrayed Death and Hades for millennia. They were below Paradise and Heaven. But just like those eternal rewards, Hades was suspended in a way where the occupants could see into Paradise and Heaven. However, the inhabitants could not leave the place to which they were sent. Residence in both domains was permanent.

The doomed souls milled about in a daze that befit their decision to follow Satan, trying to adjust to the new evil form in which they found themselves. Unlike what they saw in horror movies when they were mortal, their bodies weren't in the form of hideous monsters. They were worse. In order to inflict the most severe psychological torment for these new dark souls, Satan turned each one into the person they either loathed or were jealous of when they were alive. The walls of the orientation rooms were covered in mirrors so the new dark souls would see themselves as they entered. Satan loved the look of shock as they attempted to understand what had happened. Then, when the souls were at the height of confusion, he turned them into someone else they disliked or loathed.

Another trick Satan loved afflicting on new dark souls to increase their emotional turmoil was to confuse them. As they entered into the assembly room for their orientation into hell, each new dark soul experienced a continuation of their nightmare. He drew on their memories of what room each soul would remember as being the most uniquely feared in their mortal lives.

For some female dark souls, it was a bedroom where they were molested as a child, or beaten as a wife by a drunken husband. For some males it was a boys' locker room where they were molested by their coaches in school, or a shed where they were molested by an uncle. For others it was a car accident, or the place where they committed suicide by hanging or swallowing a bottle of their pills or cutting their wrists. Still others, it was the room where they were served divorce papers, or were handed a pink slip, or were told they were bankrupt. Another devastating reminder was the room they entered where they caught a spouse in bed with another partner. But perhaps the worst situation was for the souls who were killed as mortals in a battle in some God-forsaken war.

Then to be sure Satan compounded their pain for his maximum enjoyment, he inflicted a particular joy. In their minds Satan projected them into whatever room or place at the precise time in their lives when they each made their choice to follow him. It was not so much an overt conscious choice for Satan as their god, as it was a decision to follow the least line of resistance by doing wrong over right. In their slowly shrinking hearts, they knew where they were headed, but by the time this choice was self-evident, evil was so much a part of their lives it seemed to be the sensible choice.

Just like good begets good, so evil begets evil. Satan knew they now regretted their mortal choices, but it was too late, and he reveled in the psychological pain of them comprehending this eternal reality. So he made them go through this pain like a broken record of time, constantly repeating itself.

A third and final joy Satan used to mentally torture his new dark souls was to cement in their minds those final seconds just before death, that moment of transition from living as a human to passing into the next life where they realized they were going to hell. Once in Death and Hades, this transition played over and over in their conscious states. Now they each had their own private little hell.

For millennia, Satan used to immediately set the souls on fire so he could watch them squirm and wiggle as they burned without hope of having their flames extinguished. However, Satan soon bored with their writhing in pain. After all, burning like a torch always ended with the same results. So he came up with this plan for each soul to have his town unique personalized hell. Besides, Satan could burn them like torches any time he wanted.

After a few minutes, or perhaps a century, a dark soul much larger, uglier, and scarier than the new recruits could ever imagine, entered the room. An aura of power surrounded him. First one, then another, then all the initiates fell to their knees. Intuitively they knew he was their master, the Chief Demon.

Orientation to Death and Hades

This malevolent soul looked different to each of the thousands of new dark souls. Panic spread, terror erupted, and cries emerged as some ran and searched for a place to hide. Others shrieked as they fell down on the floor in catatonic fits of fear. This universal madness occurred because to every new recruits, this senior dark angel looked like the person each feared the most.

To some, he was the abuser, sexual deviant, or tormentor who'd made their lives as children in the flesh a living hell. To other souls, he looked like the abusive or alcoholic husband. To a few of the male souls he looked like the castrating wife they had spent decades with in lifeless marriages. Finally, to others he looked like that boss from hell. Regardless of the face or from what part of their lives it came, the figure struck terror where their hearts once resided.

All of a sudden, there was a silent hush in the large crowd. The only noises were the screams of the souls already in the pit where they were burning for eternity. They could be seen through the glass floor begging for someone to give them a least a drop of water to ease their agony. The dark souls in the burning pit were like a bunch of crabs caught at the seashore and placed in a large galvanized bucket. Each one tried to climb the sulfur laden walls to escape the fire and brimstone. However, as they reached the top, a darker, jealous soul below would pull them down into Satan's eternal caldron. Their howls sent shivers down the spines of the new recruits.

As the Chief Demon slowly edged toward the front of the orientation room, he slid by like a massive dark slug, leaving a slimy, gooey trail behind him. The stench from the goo was overpowering, like decaying corpses atop a foul garbage dump.

When he reached the front of the class he commanded the new recruits to all face forward. Some did not, however, because like in any crowd, there are always a few who are so selfish they believe their need to chat is more important than the group.

What happened next was unimaginable.

The Chief demon opened his mouth as wide as the Grand Canyon. A sucking noise spewed from the chasm. Those new recruits whose backs were toward him were sucked into his open mouth, as if he was an enormous grouper fish. Everyone in the room shrieked as hundreds of dark souls already trapped inside his body begged and screamed to be released. Then, like an anaconda swallowing its prey whole, the Chief Demon sucked the five disobedient souls from the classroom down his slimy gullet.

He licked his chops as though he were a lion on the Serengeti Plains enjoying a fresh kill. After a gurgling belch, he withdrew a toothpick made from a human bone, and pried the dark souls' remains from between his broken and uneven teeth.

The Chief Demon surveyed the room. The wide-eyed stares of the recruits reflected their shock at witnessing spiritual cannibalism. Like a drill sergeant, he bellowed, "Don't you remember the sign above the door as you entered this room? Let me remind you." He yanked a large silver platter out of thin air and held it up with both hands. The words were written in blood.

Welcome to Death and Hades,
The Home of Satan's Prime Cuts,
Thank you for Your Poor Choices While in the Body.

Every soul before him was as silent as a graveyard at midnight. They were shaking so hard that if they were in human form, their teeth would have rattled.

A sadistic smile spread across his face. "Now you know why the exclamation point at the end of the welcome sign is in the shape of a butcher knife."

A murmur arose from the crowd.

The Chief Demon then scowled so hideously no mask on Halloween could match it. He marched up and down the rows of dark souls, inspecting each one for the slightest imperfection. Periodically he would pause in front of a new recruit. The initiate that caught his eye would tremble as if he were about to be eaten. The Chief Demon sensed the soul's fear like a bear smelling its prey. He leaned over into the initiate's face, nose to nose, and growled.

Then, to the eternal relief of the one who escaped his wrath, the Chief Demon walked on to the next soul in line.

Orientation to Death and Hades

Once he had inspected every new recruit and achieved his goal of intimidation, the Chief Demon strode to the front of the class and stepped onto the stage. "My name is Durrell, your master and destroyer. You are probably wondering what happened to those five new recruits. Well, they tasted as sweet as young lambs. Let their fate be an essential lesson to you. Mistakes are not tolerated."

Durrell paced with his hands behind his back.

"Perhaps this would be a good opportunity to present your first lesson. Our Absolute Holiness of Evil watches at all times. His eyes are everywhere. He knows every move you make and every word you say. Should you commit one mistake, no matter how small, you will be hurled straight into the eternal pit over which you are standing. If I, or any other instructor, witness your mistake, you will be swallowed whole. Remember your five classmates?"

The expressions of dread on the recruits' faces brought happiness to Durrell's heart that only a condemned soul could appreciate. At first, the fear produced a slight scent which soon developed into a delicious aroma. Durrell inhaled, smacked his lips and salivated like a dog preparing to eat a bone. The aroma of fear morphed into an orange-colored gooey substance which he chewed like candy. Like a carnivore devouring a kill, he growled if any of the new dark souls approached his feast. At the awful sound erupting from his throat, every recruit sprang backward in eternal fear.

"Now I want to make a second point in this orientation. Your mommies and daddies are not here to bail you out. Some of you were so spoiled by your enabling parents and families. But that won't work here. *You* mess up, *you* suffer the consequences. While you were in that ghastly smelly body of flesh, you made your choice for Satan. Therefore, you have to live with that decision eternally in the spirit. Any questions?"

Not a sound from his audience. Good. They knew he meant business.

"Here's my third point so listen carefully. From this moment forward there are words you *will* erase from your minds and vocabulary. These are forbidden words. Never even think them, much less verbalize them. Remember, our Most Holy Evil One knows your thoughts—a valuable tip to keep in mind now that you are in his domain."

Durrell marched to the chalkboard and ran his fingernails down the length of it. The dark souls cringed.

"Do you like that sound? No? Then remember that the use of these words has the same effect on us. And should you survive your training, they will affect you the same way too."

Durrell strutted in front of the class. How he relished his role. "In your previous hideous life where you resided in that smelly body, you had freedom of choice. Well, here there is only one choice. His choice. All other choices will be punished. Here are the words never to be spoken from this moment forward. Forgiveness. Mercy. Grace."

As he spoke each word, he writhed and ached with pain. It was as though he were at a dentist having a root canal without anesthetic.

"Love. Compassion. Justice."

Periodically he had to pause because the words cut his lips and tongue as he pronounced each syllable.

"Patience. Longsuffering."

Several recruits pointed to the souls trapped inside his grotesque body that seemed to be given a little more freedom at each word uttered. It was as though the words provided an exit from his dark interior.

"Tolerance. Kindness. Hope."

Again and again, he had to use his hands to push the fleeing souls back down inside his mouth and body.

"Promise."

One lost soul nearly escaped as the last word edged out over his bleeding lips. But the Chief Demon grabbed him by his waist and pushed him down inside his mouth and swallowed. A raucous burb followed.

Durrell collapsed on the floor in a heap. He huffed and puffed with such velocity and intensity that a swarm of black, swirly clouds developed over the class. Lightning and thunder preceded a rain shower. But as the instructor caught his breath, the storm cleared, and heat from below filled the room.

With a mighty shudder, the Chief Demon attempted to stand. Uttering those unholy words was always perilous. To him and the other demons, they were a viral infection that if not tempered, could commit them to the pit.

One of the new recruits ventured forward and grabbed Durrell's arm to help him stand. But instead of offering gratitude, the Chief Demon stuffed the recruit into his mouth and swallowed him whole. He chuckled as he recalled a nature movie he once saw where a great white shark leaped out of the ocean and grabbed a seal, swallowing it in one gulp.

After Durrell swallowed the new recruit, he set his hands on his hips. "Let this be a lesson to you all. Never do anything good for others. Don't think of offering aid to anyone. No matter how you find souls, let them wallow in their filth. These acts are evil to us here in this most unholy sanctuary of pain and torment. Got it?"

Not a word was uttered by any of the recruits. Durrell smirked. Yup. They were afraid they'd be eaten too.

The Chief Demon then said, "Before I move on, are there any questions?"

No one uttered a peep.

"What words are we *not* to speak?" Durrell asked.

Several of the new dark recruits began to recite the list of words. All of a sudden, the Chief Demon opened his mouth wide. The souls of the past whom he had eaten plus the newly swallowed recruits all begged to be released. Arms outstretched and fingernails clawing at the sides of his mouth and throat, they yelled blood curdling screams and waved their arms in panic. In the midst of a swirling tornado, the ones who had made the mistake of saying the forbidden words were promptly eaten.

Again Durrell picked his teeth with a human bone, and burped. The rank odor of his belch caused a few of the closest recruits to vomit. Under his breath he murmured, "Hmm. One of those was chunky, but anther slid down as smooth as a creamy custard."

Wiping scraps of food and slime from his mouth, he pointed to the class. "Let that be another lesson to the rest of you. Didn't I tell you to *never* repeat those words?' He patted his belly. "Some of you weren't listening. Maybe now you will pay close attention to what I say."

Durrell cleared his throat and stood with his feet apart. "While we are on the subject of forbidden words, I have three more to add to the list. These are the most important, the most fearful of all." He whispered, "Father. Son. Holy Spirit."

He sucked in a deep breath and immediately looked down. Would he be cast into the fiery pit below?

The walls of the orientation room rumbled. Its glass foundations trembled. Lava from the molten earth in the pit boiled and spewed up throughout the rivers of fire.

Meanwhile, Durrell writhed in agony. The pain was more severe than he could remember. This time, no misguided recruit offered him help.

Finally, he was able to talk. "Oh, Your Most Lowliness. Your Most Despicable. Please forgive me. I'm in a classroom orientating new dark recruits."

The volcanic rumble settled down. Forgiven. For now.

With a grunt, Durrell heaved himself upright. "The next point in this orientation is that we use the sign of the cross whenever we greet each other, at the beginning and conclusion of meetings, and at the end of any prayer to our Most Lowest of the Low. However, there's a caveat. We make the sign of the cross backwards. Start by touching your right shoulder, then your left. Next, touch your midsection, and finally your forehead. Any questions?"

Again, no response.

He nodded. "Okay now everyone, practice."

As the group of novices practiced the backward signage, some disappeared into the pit below. They had made the sign of the cross incorrectly. First, only two or three departed, but the final number reached a score.

Orientation to Death and Hades

Durrell grinned. Their screams when they hit the pit of fire were music to his ears.

"When are you recruits going to learn? Don't you realize that everything I tell you is of vital importance? When you don't make this sign correctly, you insult His Excellency the Most Diabolical, The Greatest Liar in history."

The rest of the class worked extra hard to make the sign correctly. Durrell thumped his chest. No other new recruits' souls were lost to mistakes.

Although disappointed, he continued with his instructions. "There is a song you have to learn. We sing it before and after every meeting, and when we worship our Demonic Entrapper. The tune is based on a Christian song, but obviously, we have different lyrics."

He glanced around. "Before I sing the Christian song, I need to formally request the forgiveness of our Eternal Captor." He bowed his head. "Please, O Master, forgive this your humble servant for what I am about to sing because I know it goes against the evil core of where your heart beats. Amen."

As if waiting for immediate punishment, he paused. When nothing happened, he opened his mouth and sang.

In the blink of an eye, the pillars of hell rumbled. Durrell's voice rose above the commotion. Then the foundations shook. Uttering the name of Jesus caused the very gates of hell to tremble.

Durrell concluded the song and examined his extremities. He was still whole.

He stretched out his arms to the class. "Now I will plug in our lyrics. Learn them well." His voice reached the rafters and swirled around the new recruits.

"I have decided to follow Satan,
I have decided to follow Satan,
I have decided to follow Satan,
I lost my soul,
I lost my soul."

> "Finally, be strong in the Lord and in his mighty power. Put on the full armor of God so that you can take your stand against the devil's schemes."
>
> EPH 6:10, 11

> "Therefore, put on the full armor of God, so that when the day of evil comes, you may be able to stand your ground, and after you have done everything, to stand. Stand firm then, with the belt of truth buckled around our waist, with the breastplate of righteousness in place, and with your feet fitted with the readiness that comes from the gospel of peace as a firm footing. In addition to all this, take up the shield of faith, with which you can extinguish all the flaming arrows of the evil one. Take the helmet of salvation and the sword of the spirit, which is the word of God."
>
> EPH 6:13-17

13

How to Use Your Swords to Capture Souls

After a brief pause, the Chief Demon said, "Your orientation to Death and Hades is now concluded. Any questions before we proceed to the use of your sword?"

One brave new recruit held up his hand. It shook so hard that his fingers looked like the propeller blades of a helicopter.

"You there. What is your question?"

"Your Magnificence—"

A shrill howl echoed throughout all of Death and Hades. Durrell fell to the floor. "Your Most Low, Hateful One. I will address the violation immediately. Thank you for not sending both of us to the Lake of Fire."

In the blink of an eye, the new recruit was swallowed whole. The Chief Demon wiped his mouth, and commanded, "*Never* use names of honor reserved for our Most Holy Liar when you address me. Use my name, and only my name."

Another recruit shuffled forward and raised his hand. "Durrell, sir, why . . . why do we need swords?"

The Chief Demon stomped across the stage, gritting his teeth and swinging his arms. "Don't you listen to anything you're told?" He stopped and pointed to the class. "Do you think you're here on vacation? Get with the program. While on earth, you chose to follow Satan. So now he will use you to gather new souls for his kingdom, to be his soldiers. And all warriors need weapons. Those who survive the training will return to earth where you will fight the Angels of Light."

Durrell ducked and covered his head, but no crushing blows followed. He never knew when Satan would punish him for speaking of their eternal enemies.

"If you're victorious over your adversary, then we'll welcome a new dark soul into our midst." He nodded toward another recruit who held up his hand. "You have a question?"

"Yes, sir, Durrell." The initiate swallowed and paled. "Please explain the eating of souls."

"Our Most Disgusting Imminence has promised me, and others like me, that if we eat souls we will be spared from the Lake of Fire."

Taking another step forward, the recruit asked, "But Durrell, sir, how can you trust the Greatest Deceiver of all time, his Most Unforgiving Tyrant?"

Nails from Bullets

"I don't trust him, and he knows it. He doesn't trust me either. We don't believe in trust. Our relationship, like all other relationships in this place, is based on hate and deception. We do our best to cause each other to fail, or to be sent into the Lake of Fire. But the more souls I eat allows me to dine well and stay out of the Lake of Fire. So I plan to lie as best I can, eat souls, and trick novices like you for as long as I'm able."

The recruit backed away and hung his head.

Durrell smirked. "Let's begin. As you entered, you will have noticed there were no name tags or other little goodies to make you feel welcome. That's because I don't want to know your names. I don't want to be your friend. I have no desire to be close to any of you. The only thing I want is to eat as many of you as possible."

The whole group shrank backward. But they couldn't escape.

"Those of you who survive will become like me. And the more you become like me, the longer you will delay going into the Lake of Fire."

One new recruit raised a trembling hand. "Durrell, sir, isn't it true one day we will all be cast into the Lake of Fire?"

There was always one who had to ask that question. "Yes." He waited for his answer to reach into every soul. "But I believe the longer I can stay out of the burning inferno by eating fools such as you, that Diablo, the One and Only, will discover a way to prevent our eternal damnation."

When he could sense that his words had been digested, Durrell held up a book. "Open your training manual to the first page where you will find our Mantra. Each of you will memorize the words so that when you're called upon, you'll be able to recite it without thinking. You've seen our punishment for not obeying orders. Follow as I read."

Pages rustled as the recruits each opened his book.

"I swear by the stench of hell to be strong in Satan and in his supreme power. I will wear his full armor that I may resist our sworn quarry's invitation to freedom in that most unholy of unholy places. For I know my struggle is not against these worthless imbecilic humans because their souls supply my daily sustenance.

No. My struggle is against the God of Light, and his Son, our archenemy. I curse him and his despicable spirit. I will destroy them both. And finally, I am dedicated to the destruction of heaven's sniveling angels. They are so weak that they do his bidding without trickery or lies. Therefore, I will always wear the full armor of Satan. When I take my daily stand to defeat man in battle, I alone will be lauded and praised because of my power. I will wear the Belt of Lies to trick and deceive the flesh and blood quarry. I will put on the Breastplate of Corruption that I might strike at his heart of false joy. I will wield the Shield of Doubt so that from the beginning, my human contact will question his faith. I will wear the Helmet of Damnation which will deafen me to the false lies of forgiveness. But most of all, I will sharpen my Sword of Temptation to a razor's edge, for it is my greatest weapon to harvest souls."

The Chief Demon surveyed the room. A thousand pair of eyes focused on him. "You must memorize our mantra within the time frame I command. You may have a few hours or a century. Since there's no such thing as time here, you'd better get busy. Any questions?"

Again, not a word from his new recruits.

"Next, I need to discuss your weapons. Those who survive our new recruit training will be taught how to use a sword. Your mission is to win souls for Satan. If you're able to win a Christian soul, you'll earn a special medal from Satan himself. When I think you're ready, you will return to earth to begin your service for our Master."

Excited murmurs erupted from the crowd.

"There is nothing more deadly than a demon with a Sword of Vice. You must keep the blade razor-sharp at all times. Your weapon will only be used for the procurement of souls, and never for your defense. You must keep it by your side at all times, ready for use at a moment's notice."

The Chief Demon puffed out his chest. How did he get so lucky?

"The Sword of Vice is the most valuable weapon in all creation. They do not belong to you. We are only lending the swords to you. Remember, they belong to our Master. Due to their tactical worth, there are seven rules that govern their use." Durrell pointed to the chalkboard where words appeared, written in blood.

"The first rule. Your sword must become one with you. Second. It is an extension of your evil. Third. Every strike from the sword is a blow for your Master. Fourth. Your sword is your life. Fifth. It is more valuable than you are. Sixth. You will never retreat or leave your sword behind. Seventh. If you run from the enemy or drop our sword, you will be hurled straight into eternal damnation."

Durrell pointed to a recruit in the front row, and asked, "What kind of sword will you be given?"

Trembling, the dark soul said, "The Sword of Vice."

"Good. You were listening. Now let me explain why it bears that name. The sword is an instrument of evil, lies, and deception. It is to be used in any way necessary for betrayal, trickery, or corruption."

When he could tell by the expressions on the faces closest to him that the recruits were beginning to understand their role, Durrell continued.

"Next we'll move to tactics. The best strategies to steal souls are to manipulate three of humanity's basic needs. I will provide them for you in order of priority—sex, money, power. Bear in mind, these needs are not inherently evil. They are no different than the need for food, shelter, water, and clothing. Your mission is to corrupt the reason man fulfills these needs, to cause him to make a major paradigm shift. You can accomplish this strategy by guiding his heart to the selfish fulfillment of these needs, especially by demeaning other people. Are there any questions?"

His tone suggested he wouldn't tolerate any interruption.

His audience took the hint.

"Good. Our next step is to introduce you to your sword."

Was that a murmur of ridicule? Durrell studied the group. No, must have been his imagination. Who would question him introducing a sword as if it were a person?

How to Use Your Swords to Capture Souls

"Hold up your left hand and splay out your fingers." He demonstrated. "We use our left hands because in that other place," he pointed upward, "and in earthly literature, the right hand is a symbol of strength."

Durrell observed the sea of recruits. Some extended their arms and hands quickly, while others reached out tentatively as if they were afraid.

As soon as all trainees had their left hands extended, swords appeared, swooping down toward the dark souls. Durrell loved how their eyes bugged out.

The swords settled in each hand, but were so heavy, none of the students could hold them up for long. Not matter how much they struggled, their arms quivered under the weight, and all the swords drifted to the ground. However, another surprise was in store for the class. Several recruits had to let go of their swords, but the weapons did not clatter to the floor. No. They stood up on their points, as if they were standing at attention in the army. Those souls who did not let go of the hilts, found their swords in the same position—stuck in the ground.

Durrell scanned the room like a hawk until he finally found what he was looking for.

He pointed and barked, "All of you, put your hand on your sword."

Several trainees in the room could not hold onto their swords. Each time they tried to grab the hilts, the swords jumped out of their hands and threw themselves, point first, into the ground as if possessed by demons. When the recruits attempted to grab them again, the weapons moved evasively, always one step ahead of the dark souls in pursuit.

Some foolish trainees struggled to grab their swords with both hands. Big mistake. When their right hands touched the hilts they were burned. A couple of trainees attempted to wrestle their swords to the ground, but each time any part of their bodies touched the swords, they burst into flames. Several burning recruits were tossed into the Lake of Fire and Hades.

Finally, the trainees who couldn't hold onto their swords realized they were losing the battle. There was nothing they could do but stand at attention with their reluctant swords facing them as if in defiance.

Durrell strode across the stage, hands on his hips. "Let this next demonstration be a lesson permanently seared into your memories."

Immediately all the trainees whose swords refused to be held were consumed by flames. Their agonizing screeches filled the room. They writhed in pain, then their bodies rose and swirled above the rest of the recruits.

Mouths agape, the rest of the trainees did nothing but watch in horror.

The bodies of those few whose swords refused to be held were gathered into a single ball of flames, followed by a massive explosion. When the smoke cleared, there was no sign of the trainees who were burned. There was not even a pile of ash or a puff of smoke. The room was as clear of their demise as though they never existed.

The trainees standing with their swords in front of them quivered in fear. Durrell knew they were wondering if they would be next.

He chuckled. What fun. "You just witnessed the eternal damnation of those dark souls whose swords sniffed out they were not worthy of carrying them into battle. There's no point in training students who can't cut the mustard. There is no deceiving your swords. You don't need to know what happened to those recruits. All you need to know is that if you fail any part of your training, your sword will know. So bear this bit of advice in mind. Any questions?" Again his tone brooked no argument.

Durrell smirked and pointed to the class. "Hold up your sword with your left hand only. Do not attempt to use your right hand. It's going to take time for your left arm and hand to develop the strength necessary to wield this sword."

Surveying the group, Durrell nodded. Yup. He witnessed the same phenomenon he'd seen in every class he'd taught for

How to Use Your Swords to Capture Souls

thousands of years. Each sword hilt began to merge in darkness with each trainee's left hand as if grafted together.

Then there was the characteristic jolt each trainee experienced as the union was accomplished. Durrell laughed so hard, his soul-filled belly jiggled. No matter how many times he'd seen the swords and trainees fused as one, it always saturated him with mirth.

Durrell clasped his hands behind his back and paced. "Next, an electric shock will surge through your bodies. It's so painful you'll think your eyes will pop out of your souls. Well, they won't. You'll feel like a downloading computer because the sword has a record it is transferring to you. Your sword is thousands of years old, and has seen a myriad of owners. Each fight against a heavenly angel warrior has been recorded. As each dark warrior suffered defeat and was cast into the Lake of Fire, the sword passed this record on to the next owner."

Taking a deep breath, the Chief Demon added, "The history of the sword will give you a distinct advantage—it will be your leverage in every battle. This is why the rules of these swords are so strict. They will outlast everyone in here." He pointed to the students. "Eventually, you are all going to hell. It's just a question of how long you can delay the inevitable."

Durrell cackled, shaking the swallowed souls so much they writhed inside his belly. He relished telling each class these words of doom.

"In my history—I've been here a long, long time—no trainee who became an experienced soul collector has ever escaped." This time when he laughed, the borders of hell shook.

After he calmed down, Durrell continued, "These swords look like they originated in the Middle Ages. Wrong. They go back beyond my time, and their form changes. As man's history progresses, so does the appearance of these swords. But," he narrowed his eyes, "their souls, yes I said their souls, have remained the same."

Oohs and aahs escaped from some of the recruits' gaping mouths. The reaction never surprised Durrell.

"I know, I know. Swords with souls. I'm not privy to the details, but I'll share what I can. These swords predate me, back to the time when our Holy Master of Death and Darkness was cast from heaven. It is said these are the swords of all the fallen angels that accompanied him on his damned journey. Then, one by one, as the dark angles lost their battles while fighting for human souls and were thrown into Death and Hades, their swords were handed down to future generations of dark souls." Durrell jumped off the stage and pointed a bony finger into the face of the nearest trainee who shriveled into a ball. "You should feel honored to be holding one of the original swords of the fallen angels thrown out of heaven."

In a blink of an eye, he stood on the stage again, chest out, muscles bulging. "Any questions?"

By now the trainees knew the drill. They remained silent.

"Ready for your next weapon?" He didn't wait for a response. "Bend your right arm, elbow at your waist, and hold out your hand."

As soon as the trainees obeyed, a shield matching their swords appeared in their hands. The face of each shield depicted a likeness of Satan. Not his real visage because no one knows what he looks like. Each portrayal represented a characterization humans have had of Satan since Adam and Eve. On some shields a hideous snake coiled to strike. On others goat bodies pranced around with demonic heads. A few shields displayed bulls and centaurs standing upright, clad in ancient warrior clothing.

Durrell danced on the stage. He loved this part of the training. "Your shields and swords are inextricably entwined. The sword will take the lead in battle, while your shield will follow its orders to protect you." He held his arms up. "Display your weapons. You should feel invincible. No angel from heaven can defeat you."

Consenting mumbles rose from the students.

The Chief Demon lowered his arms. "It's now time to practice, you slimy ex-humans. You have to learn how to take souls for your Master and Keeper in hell. Most of you will be cast into the Lake of Fire during your first battle. Some of you will survive." He gloated at their confused expressions. "Let's see who can bite the bullet." A sadistic laugh shook Durrell's belly as he glared at his intended victims.

"All right, useless bags of trash, spread out with plenty of distance between you and the spirits around you."

The trainees obeyed.

Durrell cleared his throat. "Hold your shield in front of you and your sword straight up over your left shoulder." He demonstrated although he had no weapons. "Make believe there is an angel from heaven in front of you. Swing down and up. Down and up, as if slashing through their bodies. Each time you swing or thrust, you are tempting your intended target soul to sin. Remember, your overall goal is to tempt him to the point he gives his soul to our Ancient Father of Darkness. The angel hopes that his human will chose virtue over vice. Your fight is not against the Spirit of God—you would never win against him. Your battle is against the spirit of the man whose soul you are tempting."

The recruits grunted and groaned as they practiced his instructions.

In spite of the trainees' exhaustion, Durrell continued with his lecture. "Now I will show you how to use sex, the first of man's basic needs, to sway the target soul to our Father of Lies. Bring down your sword as hard as you can as if you want to cut your opponent into two vertical pieces." He sliced through the air with his arm. "That downward swing is vice. Your opponent will block with a parry of virtue. Now slash your sword parallel to the midsection of your opponent as if you're going to cut him in half horizontally." Again he demonstrated. "That swing is pornography. Your adversary counters with a parry of closing down the pornographic web site which the human accidently opened." Durrell chuckled. "Your target doesn't know it was not an accident."

He watched the recruits practice the methods he described. Pretty good, so far.

"Next, you parry diagonally from right to left with adultery. Your sword makes a small cut along your heavenly adversary's chest. Now you know your target soul's weakness. The disgusting angel from heaven steps back surprised, injured, and then boldly returns into the fray with his parry of honesty. You counter with your target's denial about the mutual sexual attraction with a pretty young married female coworker."

Durrell's lips twitched as he smirked. "Your human victim habitually deceives himself in his motives to find copious reasons to be near her desk, so you continue to fight. Now you are winning. Each swipe of your blade pushes your enemy angel back farther and farther. All he can do is hold his blade up in defense to protect himself against your repeated blows. He is losing this single combat because your target lies to his wife about the reason for staying late at work. The human never admits he's with a female coworker."

Satisfied that the trainees were obeying his instructions, Durrell jumped off the stage, swishing his left arm back and forth as if he held a sword. "Your human has revealed his weakness. Woohoo! To maximize your advantage, swing your blade back and forth in the shape of an X. Repeat the maneuver over and over until your target begins an affair with the young admiring female." He leaped back on the stage and completed a few backward flips. Vice trumped virtue so often.

"Your opponent will attempt to parry with anything he can find in your target's life history. For example, the heavenly warrior parries with your target's ten-year marriage, or with his two children, aged eight and six. But you continue to deflect with lust, the thrill of the chase, and excitement of getting away with something evil but which feels so good. Your challenger parries with the fact the human is a deacon in his church, and serves on several church committees."

Unable to contain his excitement, Durrell ran across the stage, whooping and hollering. "Never mind what your adversary uses to block your thrusts because now you are winning. Therefore, you can slice again and again. The wife suspects her husband and senses a distance between them. You continue to parry by making him think he no longer loves his wife and is in love with his adulteress. Wield your sword to make their passion so strong they both feel they no longer love their respective spouses. The adulteress has been married twelve years and has three children. No big deal. Swing your sword faster and faster so that they are willing to throw their families away."

Out of breath, Durrell sat on the edge of the stage. "By this time, you have your opponent on the ground. Your sword thrusts revealed deceit and lasciviousness as the primary ingredients in the adulterous couple's relationship, vices they are not even aware of. Next will come the coup de grace—when the adulterous couple leave their respective families and move in together."

Refreshed, he jumped up and strode the length of the stage. "It doesn't matter if they stay together or not. Most of these types of relationships don't last. Your goal of taking his soul will eventually be achieved because he crossed this forbidden boundary. And like all boundaries, once crossed the first time, they become easier to cross again and again."

Durrell allowed the recruits time to process his words. He paced back and forth for eons, then asked, "Class, do you have the hang of it?" But he really didn't want to know.

"Since there are no questions, it's now time for you to practice using mankind's weaknesses of money and power on your own. I will circle the room to watch and offer advice."

Taking pride in the fact he was not the typical encouraging type of teacher, the Chief Demon preened. He acted more like a critical, controlling parent looking for the smallest mistake. Yup. He accomplished this with absolute perfection. Some members of the class were slow to grasp the concepts he spewed. They received the focus of his sharp tongue.

He stopped to catch his breath in the passing moments or centuries, depending on how one viewed time outside the realm of Death and Hades. Thus revived, he became worse than the meanest drill instructor on earth.

"What's wrong with you idiots? Don't you have a brain? You all disgust me. Do I have to do everything? What vice will allow you to use money to lure your victims from God?"

There was an immediate hush in the room. Durrell suspected the recruits were too afraid to say anything. They knew the possible punishment—flung into the Lake of Fire prematurely.

Finally, one brave dark soul hesitantly stepped forward. "Is it greed?"

Durrell thumped a fist into his palm. "Exactly. You must plant a seed of greed in your victim's heart. And how pray tell do you do this, trainee?"

Having dared to answer the first question, the dark soul recruit scratched his head. "I guess one way we can do it is to start when the target soul is young. Make the family poor so they lead a hard life. The young soul grows up determined to be rich. He accomplishes his goal, but in the process, instead of accumulating resources to provide for his needs, stockpiling wealth takes over. Hoarding becomes his god."

"Excellent. What else happens?"

Now the novice recruit seemed embolden. He thrust out his chest. "The target soul works long hours, saves to excess, accumulates possessions to the extent that what he owns means more to him that the people around him. His wife leaves him, and his children abandon him. They seek revenge because decades earlier he abandoned his role of father and husband." The recruit stepped forward. "He didn't attend his kids' extracurricular activities, acknowledge their academic prowess, nor be part of their athletic activities. And he treats his wife more like a roommate than a life mate."

Durrell pranced like a proud peacock spreading his tail feathers to attract the hens. Yes. This recruit got it. What a student. "Good for you. You've hit the nail on the head. The use of these subtle facets of greed during the target soul's life-journey of gaining wealth is crucial. *He* will try to convince himself that he's doing it all this for his family. When in truth, he's building a financial empire as his god. Greed has become his all-consuming deity." He jutted his chin toward the recruit. "Now get back with the other sorry souls."

Without warning, all the swords and shields lowered to the ground and stood upright in front of their recruits. The dark souls rubbed their aching muscles.

"I see it's time for us to move on to the last part of your training. We're going to explore your identified target's three key weaknesses. Listen closely as I explain what they are. They will be the most effective tools in your tool chest of corruption and vice."

All of a sudden, words in crimson appeared on the chalkboard.

Three Greatest Weaknesses of a Target Christian's Soul

Durrell folded his arms across his broad chest. "Although your target soul belongs to a person who calls himself a Christian, he relies more heavily on himself than his God."

A commotion interrupted him. A recruit pushed through to the front and waved his hand. "I have a question, sir."

Durrell rolled his eyes. How he hated to be interrupted, but it might be important. "What is it?"

"Are we only going after Christian souls?"

"Yes, you knucklehead. All the other souls already belong to us. Back to my lecture. Instead of developing a relationship with Christ, you target soul thinks safety lies under the umbrella name of Christian. Strategically, this is his key weakness, and never forget it. Hence, you will exploit it for his downfall. Cognitively, he knows his strength is not enough to resist temptation. He also knows without a strong spiritual life he is at greater risk to your vice's temptation. But there are three reasons he does not spend the time necessary to strengthen his spiritual life. Do you want to know what they are?"

Trainees cheered and stomped their feet. The roar filled Durrell with pride. He pointed to the board and words emerged under the heading already in place.

First, the Christian's prayer life is weak.

"The Christian knows he should pray more when he is in a jam, but he is too busy. So his prayer life is placed on the back burner until he finds time to pray. This rarely happens, of course. Ironically, he discovers he has an abundance of time to pray when he is going through an emergency or tragedy. Then he beats himself up with guilt."

Sneering, the Chief Demon strode across the stage. "Here is where you have another great inroad to employing your temptation even deeper into his spiritual weakness."

He jabbed his thumb over his shoulder. More words appeared on the board.

Second, use the Christian's guilt against him.

"Let's examine the next weakness. Your target soul already feels guilty because he doesn't have a sustained prayer life. And by a sustained prayer life, I mean one that he looks forward to each day, one that evolves to where he prays all day every day, like we do here in Death and Hades." Durrell bowed his head. "Praised be His Imminence of Injustice. For you see when you target soul prayed in the past he did so out of obligation and duty, not due to devotion and communion with his Father. Praised be His Majesty of Cruelty."

The Chief Demon sat on the edge of the stage. As much as he enjoyed instructing the trainees, it sure sapped his energy.

He sighed and rubbed his neck before continuing. "So out of guilt the human will make feeble attempts to begin a prayer life. He might feel better because he is praying more. But here's his mistake that we will use to our advantage. During his endeavor, guilt will engulf him because he didn't pray much before his emergency. Then, when the emergency does not resolve itself immediately, or when he thinks it should, guilt will overwhelm his soul, and he'll blame himself."

Unable to keep still, Durrell stood and paced. "Don't think that's the end for your target soul. Oh, no. He translates the guilt into believing that his God is punishing him. Suits us fine. Now he either sinks deeper into guilt, or he becomes angry and gives up his God."

The demon punched his fist into the air. "Either way, we have his soul. He's looking for immediate spiritual gratification. Big mistake. He doesn't have enough spiritual depth to understand that prayer is for the long haul." Again, Durrell bowed his head. "Hail to his Eternal Glory."

After clearing his throat, he said, "Your target soul doesn't grasp that not only his prayer life, but his entire life is in his Father's hands. Hence, his God works at his own speed, and not when the help is requested. As you can see, the soul's guilt deepens at each step. Hence, he gives up and contemplates abandoning God to join us. Why? Because he thinks his God doesn't care. Here again he does not grasp the irony that his God does care, it's *our* god who doesn't give a hoot."

Energized, Durrell danced across the stage and pointed to the board where more words appeared.

Third, use his ignorance of the Bible against him.

"Here is the final weakness we'll discuss. Your target human doesn't read his God's word very often. He complains he doesn't understand it. Let me ask you." Durrell surveyed his audience. "Is this really the reason he doesn't read his Bible?"

All the recruits shook their heads.

"You're learning. Good. The answer is no. Wonder why? There are many modern translations available that are easy to read and comprehend. Use your target soul's self-deception as to why he doesn't read his God's word against him. The truth is he doesn't want to take the time to study his Bible for the same reason he doesn't want to have a steady diet of spiritual prayer with his God. He is too busy living life on earth to realize the importance of the next life. He hasn't thought through the spiritual reality that his mortal life is a preparation for his eternal life."

A whispered voice in the group caught the Chief Demon's attention. "Who dares to talk while I'm in the middle of my lecture?"

No one owned up.

"That's what I get for complementing you. Disrespect." Durrell pounced on a recruit in the second row and swallowed him, head first. He scowled at the class, daring another member to disobey him. But they disappointed him and kept quiet. He climbed back onto the stage and stuck his hands on his hips.

"I don't like to be interrupted. Breaks my train of thought. Where was I? Oh, yes. Think about it. We have a huge number of Christians in Death and Hades to this day, because they are so busy doing other things they can't find the time to read the Bible or pray. In fact, I think we have more souls down here who called themselves Christians while on earth than we have atheists" He strutted like he led a marching band, then pivoted and faced the class. "At least atheists were honest about their disbelief in God. Many of these Christians who are in denial about their faith, attended all the right church functions, and experienced all the right rituals and ceremonies only to end up here with us. See how easy it is. Even their own Bible says, 'Pride goes before destruction, a haughty spirit before a fall.'"

A recruit in the second row waved his hand at Durrell. "May I make a comment, sir?"

What's this? A trainee had something to add? How gutsy. The Chief Demon thought a moment, then nodded. "Okay."

"All of my family are Christians. They'd rather have surgery than open their Bibles."

"Exactly my point. Use that attitude for your benefit. Man's ignorance of his God's word will allow you to play all sorts of tricks on him to win him over to our god." He dipped his head and said, "May our master always rule underhandedly."

The floor didn't open up and swallow him. Sighing in relief, Durrell stared at his audience. "Much of what the Christian thinks he knows about his faith is based on what he's been told and not what he's studied for himself. Therefore, he's susceptible to atheists, agnostics, church traditions from his denomination, and other unsubstantiated beliefs."

A rumble from deep within his being halted his lecture. Ooh, that last recruit was bitter. He burped and proceeded with the training.

"The best way to exploit man's ignorance of his God's word is to appeal to his politically correct pride. When people are asked in church or around religious circles if they believe in the Bible they will say yes. However, when pressed at their jobs, or at universities, or in polite society gatherings, you will discover they only believe in select parts of the Bible. They will give the standard politically correct statements such as, the Bible was written by men, it was written a long time ago so it does not apply now, the Bible is subject to individual interpretation, and many other PC arguments."

Durrell grinned. How he loved political correctness. It made humans act in strange ways. "Men offer these replies because they don't want to be perceived as unscientific, or under-educated, or, most of all, appear out of step with people whose opinions they value. Finally, the stupid humans think their faith is satisfied with one-day-a-week worship. They don't realize worshiping their God is like worshiping Satan—it's a daily responsibility."

Murmurs of agreement rose from the class.

"But I digress. Man is not honest about the motives behind his thoughts. *That* is his greatest weakness. These wretched humans have all kinds of thoughts, many of which they know are wrong, but they don't act on them. Your goal is to discover which of the three temptations, sex, power, and money, embody his greatest weakness so he will start acting on it. And remember, you only need one. Don't be greedy and try to tempt him with more than one. Help him stay focused. Then, once you've identified his all-consuming frailty, continue to use your sword to parry with the angel protecting this human."

The Chief Demon demonstrated by swishing his arm back and forth as if he held a sword.

"Don't become discouraged if the vice doesn't tempt him immediately. It may take your human five, ten, or even fifteen years, but in the end, catching him on your hook of adultery, pornography, or pedophilia is all that matters. We're in no hurry down here. Snaring your human is all that's important. Here in Death and Hades, we have time eternal, until the God whom we despise returns."

Stepping forward, a recruit asked, "Sir, why does it take so long?"

"Why does it matter? You have nowhere else to go. Get back in line and listen." Trainees. Were any of them intelligent?

Nails from Bullets

Durrell swallowed his anger and returned to his lecture. "Remember, you are a planter of temptation's dark seeds which take time to find fertile ground. Some seeds are initially suppressed because of the responsibilities of daily life. Notice I said suppressed, not addressed. Other seeds immediately take root because of sheer luck and opportunity, however they might not be fertile. There's always a chance that the human will 'get religion'. Take your time and wait. This knee-jerk reaction will eventually fade away like a shadow." Durrell leapt into the air and landed with a thud on the stge. "Oh, I love this part. Finally, there will be a few seeds that fall on lust's fertile ground. They will produce a hundredfold, without much effort."

The same recruit who asked the last question, held up his hand.

"What do you want now?" The Chief Demon snarled.

Lowering his hand, the recruit stammered, "Durrell sir, please give us some examples."

"Sorry, I can't. This is not the time or place. If you want to learn more you'll have to attend the advanced class on temptation. But I will give you a few pointers." He cleared his throat. "When you use the temptation of sex, don't be blatant. Sexual temptation has to start subtly and quietly like a gentle brook flowing without a sound. For example, a young couple has a fight. The next morning at the office, the husband sees a bit of cleavage on a pretty female co-worker. Wait a few months to allow the young man and the woman at the office to get to know each other. Remember, men are visual creatures. They will dwell on a bit of cleavage like a kid in a candy store with no money. How's an important rule. Wanting and not having, makes the wanting stronger."

He pointed to the recruit who'd asked the question. "What's the rule?"

"Um, I can't remember."

In the blink of an eye, the recruit was sucked into Durrell's mouth. He wiped his lips and yelled, "Every word I utter is of vital importance." He bounded off the stage and grabbed a trainee by the neck. "What's the rule?"

"Wanting . . . and not having, makes the wanting stronger." The words barely made it out through his constricted throat.

Durrell dropped him to the ground where he crumbled into a heap. "Your life depends on your ability to remember my words." He roared with laughter, then sobered and continued as if nothing untoward had happened. "You might have to wait a year to reap your reward. Sometimes, the longer the better. During that time the man sees more cleavage, a brush of the hand, and an invite to lunch to talk about work."

He winked. "Or is it? Let the man have a few more fights with his young wife. Or maybe she becomes pregnant and they can no longer have sex. Now, you really have his sexual fires going. Also, if the young woman at his office is married, cause problems in her relationship with her husband. If she is not married, all the better."

The Chief Demon consulted his watch. "Class, we have to stop here. I need to teach you our Dishonorable Lord's Prayer. Etch it into your memory—you've seen what happen to recruits who forget—and recite it twice a day. I will call on you to repeat it publically. You might be thinking we have no time here to recite the prayer once, let alone twice a day."

Saliva dribbled down Durrell's chin. He swiped it away on his sleeve and grimaced at the recruits. "You all look pretty juicy to me, right about now. So pay attention. That's the point. We don't have time to stop to recite prayers, so these words better be going through your slimy little minds all the time. If they aren't, our Father will know and you will become his next prime rib supper."

His laughter bubbled up from the depths of his chubby gut. The sound echoed in the room. Recruits trembled. Good. Just the reaction he craved. He bowed his head.

> "Our Evil Father who art in Hell,
> Inglorious be thy unholy name,
> Thy dark kingdom come,
> Thy cruel will be done,
> Under earth and on earth, as it is in Hell,
> Give us this day our poor lost soul,

Nails from Bullets

And never forgive us as we will never forgive others,
Teach us how to lead humans into temptation,
That they may never be delivered from You,
For thine is the kingdom, the power and the glory,
Forever.
Amen."

Durrell lifted his head and peered into the eyes of the trainees. "You will notice our prayer is patterned after the evil one's model prayer, found somewhere in his Bible. We did this deliberately. Here in Death and Hades we want to insult him as much as we can. What better way than turning his Scriptures into one of ours?"

"Be self-controlled and alert. Your enemy the devil prowls around like a roaring lion looking for someone to devour."

I PET 5:8

"And even if our gospel is veiled, it is veiled to those who are perishing. The god of this age has blinded the minds of unbelievers, so that they cannot see the light of the gospel of the glory of Christ, who is the image of God."

II COR 4:3-4

"And no wonder, for Satan himself masquerades as an angel of light."

II COR 11:14

14

Advanced Class on Winning Souls for Satan

Durrell surveyed the class. "Do you all want to remain in this advanced class of how to win souls for Satan?"

A morbid hush engulfed the room. Fear etched on every face. The chief Demon chuckled. Yup. They were all too afraid to speak up.

"This is your final call. If you do not want to stay, speak up now." He shoved his hands on his hips and sneered at his audience.

"Master Durrell," one of the new recruits dared to talk.

"Yes, you miserable waste of dark spirit, what do you wish to ask?"

"If we don't want to be in this advanced class, where do we go, and what will happen to us?" Although he stood erect, his voice quivered.

"You will be issued a sword and forced to battle one of the hideous, disgusting angels from above to win a single soul for your Master."

Shoulders drooping, the recruit took a step backward. "Then what is the benefit of staying in this class? What happens to those of us who complete the session?"

"If you who survive this class, you will not fight with the sword. You will participate in covert activities which will influence many souls to follow our Demented Most High." Durrell focused on the soul who'd asked the questions. "You will return to the earth where those ugly thin-skinned things live, but they won't be able to see you because you will be in a different dimension. They will sense your presence, and in many instances, mistakenly blame you for evil. However, they will never guess your true mission."

Merging with the row of recruits behind him, the diminutive dark soul stammered, "What is our mission, sir?"

Durrell puffed out his chest and paced. "Your assignment will be to search for weaknesses in these slimy creatures, which you will use to convert to our Master of Ultimate Darkness. You are to accomplish your job with finesse and guile. Your manipulation will not only influence certain handpicked individuals to turn to Satan's kingdom, but influence multiple generations to follow their weak example. The souls you influence will lead thousands more to Satan over many generations, thereby increasing your success to the Dark Way multifold."

"Will there be a special reward for these covert skills?" The dark soul seemed to have regained his courage. Was his wicked

Advanced Class on Winning Souls for Satan

heart becoming accustomed to an internal sinister fascination with harming others?

"Yes there is." The Chief Demon stopped in front of the questioner. "Those souls who succeed will become part of the upper royalty of Satan's realm. They will be privy to untold powers of which I have no understanding, since I've never been able to reach such heights." Although embarrassed, he held his head high. "Let me add that there's no reward without risk, but failure will result in an eternal punishment so heinous that it has always horrified the best of us. Mark my words. Think deeply before you decide." He eyed his audience, staring into each face. "Once you make your decision, there's no turning back."

A low rumble spread though the group. Trainees stared at each other, seeking guidance.

Durrell smiled. He could almost taste their fear. He thumped his fist against the chalkboard and words appeared in large letters.

The Advanced Lecture on how to Win Souls for Satan

He pointed to the board. "It's time to begin our lecture on how to win the masses of flesh and blood creation who came from the Garden. We—"

"I have a question." A student from the second row pushed through to the front.

Seething, Durrell asked, "What is it?"

"How are we supposed to remember everything we've been taught?"

"You slime bucket. Why didn't you ask this question before you became part of the advanced class?" Durrell rolled his eyes. "Doesn't matter. Most of you will never complete this session. Attrition is one of my favorite words."

A collective groan oozed from the class. The Chief Demon danced across the stage. The power his position provided warmed the cockles of his dark heart.

"In a few minutes, you will be given devious tactics that will be branded into your brains, causing the most pain you will experience in your miserable, rotten lives. Some of you will not survive the full process. Those who fail, will fall into the Lake of Fire."

Nails from Bullets

A great howling of exquisite agony poured out from the students. The room shook, the dark souls screamed in agony as their brains were seared.

Durrell grinned. He loved how his Master had chosen to use this branding to signified his ownership of the students who would now become part of a subversive group especially trained to influence their victims to choose Satan over God. Although they were spirits, Satan allowed them to experience mortal pain because it was within his capability to alter their physical state at any time, until the second coming of Jesus. Durrell pumped his fist into the air. Hail to the Great Deceiver.

The students writhed in agony. Smoke poured from their nostrils, out of their ears and mouths as their flesh burned. But they could not die. While experiencing excruciating pain, the new students finally grasped what they had allowed themselves to be tricked into believing. Fear etched into their faces.

The Chief Demon strutted back and forth. He knew what the students were thinking. Was there more to come? Could they change their minds? No way. He harrumphed. Everything in Death and Hades was based on a lie, in one form or another.

The dark souls slowly shook off their pain and faced the front.

Durrell eyed the students. Ah, they were recovering from their first burn. Too bad. He cleared his throat. "Does anyone care to venture how best to influence man to choose Satan over God?"

No one uttered a word.

"Come on, isn't there one brave soul?"

Again, silence.

"In order for you to understand how best to influence man to choose darkness, you need to know Satan's overall game plan. There will be a second coming of Jesus when we will all be cast into the Lake of Fire. There is no way of escaping this punishment. Although you have heard me refer to a hope that Satan may escape and take some of us with him, we all know this is a lie. Hence, what we want to do is take as many of mankind with *us* as possible."

The students seemed to be paying attention. About time.

Advanced Class on Winning Souls for Satan

"You are here because we exploited your weaknesses. Other souls will follow—they will also believe Satan's lie. We are proud of our defiance and rebellion. We don't want to be in submission to any deity except ourselves. We want to be the masters of our own fate, even if this fate means we spend eternity in the Lake of Fire. We are fighting a war we know we can't win, so by hurting as many of his creation as possible, we hurt him. We gather great satisfaction in causing him the ultimate pain of loosing souls while we descend to our eternal torment."

The students settled down, and Durrell shuddered. He hated the way God's thoughts infiltrated into his mind. How dare he think he has any say in the matter when we've already chosen our fate? Puffing out his chest, he said, "Your goal will be to go to earth and search for a certain type of individual."

Silence reigned over the room. Who would ask the necessary question?

A student to the left of the stage, raised his hand. "What type of person, Durrell?"

> "To the Jews who had believed him, Jesus said, 'If you hold to my teaching, you are really my disciples. Then you will know the truth, and the truth will set you free.'"
>
> JOHN 8:31-32

> "Thomas said to him, 'Lord, we don't know where you are going, so how can we know the way?' Jesus answered, 'I am the way and the truth and the life. No one comes to the Father except through me. If you really knew me, you would know my Father as well. From now on, you do know him and have seen him.'"
>
> JOHN 14:5-7

15

Man Prefers a Complicated Lie Over the Simple Truth

Durrell smiled. He could feel his cheeks bunch. How he loved this section of his lecture. He pointed to the chalkboard and new words appeared.

Profile of the Charismatic Leader

"Do you want to know what makes the trickster successful in converting humankind to Satan?"

The audience chorused, "Yes, Durrell. Tell us, sir."

"You have to search for a person with a key personality trait. And that characteristic is charisma. A charismatic person has the power to win peoples' confidences, not so much by what he says, but by his fabricated warmth, acceptance, love, and patience. His disciples are impressed by his poise. He seems to be genuine, and his doctrines provide answers to happiness and success. With powers to hypnotize and mesmerize, his followers blindly adhere to his precepts without question."

Gathering steam, the Chief Demon marched up and down. "In order to employ his charismatic gifts, this person has to crave power and understand how he can obtain it. He has to be egocentric and narcissistic. By nature, he doesn't desire daily work or commitment to a task that requires consistent effort. All he wants is immediate gratification. Usually he is intelligent, but lacks the aspiration to develop his mental acuity. Instead, he relies on his wits and is spontaneous and impulsive."

Durrell pointed to the board again, and a new set of words appeared.

How to Mold the Charismatic Leader to Persuade Others to Follow Him

"Class, this is where you come in. Compare what I have described to the basic ingredients of a cake. Before you can bake it, you have to combine the ingredients."

Three students stepped forward, elbowing each other. Fiendish expressions beautified their countenances. Durrell purred. They were blossoming into perfect demons.

The soul in the middle asked, "Durrell, sir, how do we do this?"

"You will start slowly, maybe even taking months, perhaps years. Let your charismatic target see his power in his circle of friends. Whisper subtle suggestions of how to control two or three people with whom he associates. Let him see how easy it is for him to take the lead. Furthermore, allow him to experience how it feels to have his opinion valued above others. Top off these ingredients by finding a target who is also handsome, taller than most men, with a toned, muscular body."

Nails from Bullets

Standing mid-stage, Durrell flexed his biceps.

"Let his ego and pride fill him like a supersized air balloon, and one day, through your suggestions, he will realize he can become wealthy by establishing *the* one true church." He pumped his fists in the air, and yelled, "Whoop, whoop. We are so powerful."

After celebrating for eons, the chief Demon twirled on the stage while flinging words at the board. When he settled in front of the class, he pointed over his shoulder. "Memorize the three steps a charismatic leader must follow to create a successful cult."

A few students near the back of the room shuffled their feet and mumbled complaints. Fellow apprentices glared at them. Immediate silence. Good. Peer pressure worked every time.

Durrell snapped his fingers. All eyes focused on him. "Before I discuss these steps, there is an historical perspective you need to know. Long before Christ visited the earth over two thousand years ago, we used these same methods to establish pagan cults. So don't think they're reserved just for Christian cults."

He gazed off into the distance. "Going all the way back to Moses, the traits of successful cult leaders have always been the same—egotistical, narcissistic, vain, selfish. Once man developed large cities and city-states, pagan cults followed. Once Christ came along, all we did down here in Death and Hades was adapt what we already knew of human nature. In fact, you might say we had thousands of years to sharpen and hone our techniques through trial and error in preparation for when Christ would be born."

Durrell paused and when he reaped no repercussions for saying *the* name so many times, he smiled. "After the cross, when we discovered not even Death and Hades could defeat *him*, we began our preparation to use these techniques with *his* followers. We knew it wouldn't be long before Christians began to squabble and fight among themselves. Their infighting led them to initiate their own private brands of Christianity. Read the New Testament. There's nothing but fighting and squabbling from Matthew to Revelation."

Leaping off the stage, the Chief Demon towered over the students. "Therefore, I urge you to follow principle number one."

Man Prefers a Complicated Lie Over the Simple Truth

Instantly, the chalkboard shook and new words appeared.

Number one: Learn the Christian Bible from Genesis to Revelation so that you know it better than Christians do.

"If you want to learn how best to defeat your enemy, study the book he claims he knows. Learn it better than your Christian prey. Using this knowledge like Satan's net, you'll be able to reap a wealth of souls from the depths of Christianity's ocean. Your nets will be so full, they will flip over your boat of trickery and deceit. Your bounty will be sevenfold—so will be your reward."

He pretended to throw a ball at the board where another phrase shimmied into life.

Number two: Cain murdering Abel gave Satan insight into exploiting man's weakness of pride.

"There have always been good and bad men. Mankind has struggled between his flesh and spirit from the time of Adam and Eve. For example, we were very proud of ourselves when Cain murdered his brother Abel. We were almost more proud of this accomplishment than we were over Adam and Eve's banishment from the Garden. It's one thing to be expelled from you home for disobedience, but quite another for brother to murder brother."

He grinned. Oh, that was a delightful day.

"When we tempted Adam and Eve to defy God's prohibition about the fruit from a certain tree in the Garden, we learned then how much to whisper and suggest. Our experience came in handy when we confronted Cain. We used the knowledge to our benefit by whispering in Cain's ear, increased his jealousy, and instilled rebellion in his soul. We convinced Cain that murdering his brother Abel was his idea. Mind you, we did have to spend some time to plant the evil seed, and then make him ignore his guilty conscience."

The hairs on Durrell's neck stood to attention. Something was not right. He surveyed the class and noticed two students in the rear falling asleep. He pushed his way through the crowd, grabbed the pair, and shoved them in his mouth. They slid down his throat, screaming and cussing.

He swallowed and wiped his mouth on his shirt sleeve. "Stay awake, unless you want to complete my meal."

Shuffling feet was all he heard.

"With no more interruptions, I'll continue. This is where our craft of instilling jealously was so sharply refined. We also learned how to use jealousy to overcome guilt, anger to conquer shame, rage to prevail over disgrace, and rebellion to surmount loyalty."

Durrell drew in a deep breath. Of course, he could provide all this information digitally, but he so enjoyed the process.

"The demon assigned to Cain had a difficult time getting him to stop feeling guilty about how murdering Abel would hurt his mother. Not that Adam wouldn't also feel the loss, but he knew it would be more painful for Eve since she carried both Cain and Abel in her womb. But," he wagged his index finger in the air, "we gleaned unexpected rich knowledge about women from this successful murder that the Bible does not record. We have been using it ever since, for thousands of years."

An aspiring agent of evil waved his arm. "Durrell, sir, what did you learn?"

"I'm so glad you asked." He beamed at the student. "Mothers blame themselves when their children commit bad acts. They think there was something wrong with them, or they produced bad seed, or that they were remiss in teaching their children right from wrong."

The thought of Eve in pain and her successive generations suffering, brought such joy to where his heart once beat. He pranced and twirled like a young colt, then sighed. Back to business.

"This is where we get a two for one conversion to our Master. And if we teach you the skills just right, there's no telling how many generations of women's lives you can ruin, and in so doing, recruit them for our Supreme Being. We rejoiced tenfold when we saw how miserable they became. These female humans suffer from depression, and sometimes they commit suicide. But," he hopped off the stage, "you want to prevent this."

"Why?" The student who asked, shrunk under Durrell's gaze, but he added, "Wouldn't she think God abandoned her, and therefore turn to our Master, giving him her soul?"

"You're missing the point. Never forget my next words. Why settle for one soul when you can have so many more over several generations? You want to whisper in her heart that God has abandoned her. But you also want her to be depressed to the point of feeling suicidal, but I'll stress again. Don't let her commit suicide. Never allow her to follow through when she can become such a burden to her husband and children."

Nods of assent greeted his scan of the group. Finally, they were seeing his point.

"Let the mother use her feelings of guilt to pass along to her daughters. This way, they'll experience depression together. Redirect her guilt so you can lead her to be either exceptionally critical of her sons, or emotionally distant. Then the sons will grow up with problems in their relationships with women." Durrell paused, salivating on the concepts. "The opportunities are endless for us. We learned so much from that first murder. In the act of Cain killing Abel, Satan first saw the potential of how easy it is to create all types of lust, greed, and the need for power in mankind."

He pointed over his shoulder, and another set of words wriggled onto the board.

Number three: Man prefers a God he can see over one he can't see.

"Okay, now I must continue with the list of principals. Remember what I said earlier about knowing your enemy's battle plan better than he does?"

"Yes," the whole class responded in unison.

"Good. Turn in your Bibles to Psalm 115. King David has one meaning for his words. He wrote them as a warning about idols in his day. We, however, have an alternative interpretation to be used to our advantage that will become self-evident as I explain."

He singled out a student in the front row. "You, read verses two through eight."

Nails from Bullets

Stepping forward, the student cleared his throat and began to read, hesitantly at first, then with vigor. "Why do the nations say, 'Where is their God?' Our God is in heaven; he does whatever pleases him. But their idols are silver and gold, made by the hands of men. They have mouths, but cannot speak, eyes, but they cannot see; they have ears, but cannot hear, noses, but they cannot smell; they have hands, but cannot feel, feet, but they cannot walk; nor can they utter a sound with their throats. Those who make them will be like them, and so will all who trust in them."

"Excellent, you worthless piece of matter. Everyone, memorize these words." Durrell eyed the group. Not a murmur. Good. "There has always been an inherent trait in mankind to be a follower. That is why leaders are able to persuade so many to conform to their fold. People want someone to believe in. They want someone or something they can see, hear, smell, taste, or touch. They find it difficult believing in a benevolent being of a spiritual nature. Why do you think, almost from the beginning of time, mankind made so many idols using all sorts of materials? Even with these idols, they still had breaches of faith."

He rubbed the tight muscles in his neck. Why did Satan allow them to experience pain when they were spirits? Oh, well. Get on with the job.

"Think about that scripture. David may have been warning mankind about the false hope generated through useless idols. But what he didn't know, or perhaps did know but didn't write, he gave us a valuable piece of strategic information with which to capture and corrupt souls. If man does not find an idol in vices, he will find an idol in another human being. Either way, it's a win-win for us. We have his soul no matter which way he turns."

Students nodded.

Durrell continued, "Open your Bibles to I Samuel. Read all of chapter 8."

Some students mouthed the words, while others read out loud. The din warmed Durrell's heart. The class of potential new soul stealers seemed so enthusiastic. He gave them a few more minutes to complete the task, then asked, "What struck you as important?"

A voice rose from the middle of the group. "Verse five says, 'You,' I think he's referring to Samuel, 'are old, and your sons do not walk in your ways, now appoint a king to lead us, such as all the other nations have.'"

"What does that verse teach us about God's followers?"

The entire class responded, "Israel preferred a king over their God."

Dancing with his knees high like a marching band director, Durrell laughed. "Exactly, and man has not changed ever since."

A cheerful hum rose from the class.

Durrell marched up to the chalkboard and hit it hard. "Next, you will learn the seven pillars for starting a Christian cult."

Words wavered into focus.

First, the leader needs a new revelation that only he understands.

"By creating this unique egocentric revelation, the leader can interpret it any way he chooses. Each time he creates a new revelation, or changes a previous one, he can say the words came from God. He will have no dissenters because who will question God?"

With a flourish, the Chief Demon indicated the board, where the next set of words sprung to life.

Second, the leader will need a sacred book or books that he alleges were given to him by God.

"These books will be considered holy, and will be revered over the Bible. Herein lies the beauty of creating this book. On the one hand, the cult will say the Bible is God's work and testify to it. However, if what their cult leader has written offers a conflicting revelation, it will replace what is said in the Bible. Yet, they will have some explanation demonstrating the two conflicting statements are compatible."

Durrell slapped the board and another phrase appeared.

Third, his church is magnetically exclusive.

"What do I mean by magnetically exclusive? The cult advertises that it is open to all, however, to become a member, each person must participate in or obey some initiation ritual. Something that will draw them in, like a magnet. Usually the procedure involves contributing all or most of the adherents' personal assets. Or, they must complete courses which are exorbitant in cost. Either way, where one's money goes, so goes the person. The ritual will also offer promises of wealth, success, or power, provided the initiate is in complete obedience."

Durrell's mouth began salivating. He could hardly contain himself as he said, "This is the baited hook that brings in untold numbers of fresh fish souls."

An initiate in the back hollered, "What do you mean?"

"Mankind has an inherent need to work for and earn his salvation. This was never God's plan. At first, in the early church, Christians understood grace was free, but then one of our agents set to work. Several hundred years ago, he was able to plant in the minds of certain Christian leaders that although grace was free, it still had to be earned. He was able to whisper into their consciences and remind them of their sins, enhancing their feelings of guilt. He then nurtured and pruned this guilt until it developed into the perfect healthy plant of *deeds.* Convincing mankind that his actions are necessary for salvation has been one of our most successful tools in reaping souls for centuries."

"How does this work, Durrell?" a class initiate asked.

"Because it has grown into the spiritual cancer we so richly deserve. Millions of Christians are now serving Satan in hell because, no matter how hard they worked to demonstrate their worth to their fellows, they always slipped in some small way. They forgot that living in God's abundant grace had nothing to do with how others perceived them. In frustration, these Christians finally quit their respective churches because they could never be good enough. Then, in exasperation, they abandoned their faith, leaving them easy prey for our top agents."

The same student raised his hand. "What do you mean Durrell?"

"Christians are most vulnerable to temptation after they realize they can't be good enough to receive God's grace. Therefore,

Man Prefers a Complicated Lie Over the Simple Truth

when the three forms of temptation come along, sex, money, and power, what do you think they say to themselves?"

"We don't know," the class responded.

"The fresh meat who think they have fallen from his grace, say, 'I'm going to hell anyway, might as well enjoy it.'"

Durrell sprinted back and forth, chortling with glee. "Now we have him. He's on the line. He belongs to us. We can do anything we want to him. Divorce. Alcoholism. Adultery. The list is endless."

He wiped spittle form his lips, and continued his lecture. "I presented this history in order for you to understand who will be attracted to Christian cults. People who, for one reason or another, need to improve their self-worth. They desire a system that demonstrates they can earn their way to heaven. Think of it this way. It's like the Boy Scout's merit badges. These new fish we have on our line won't be satisfied until they have enough merit badges to become an Eagle Scout." Durrell grinned. "And of course they can't."

He faced the board and aimed his index fingers as if they were guns. He shot the next words out of both barrels.

Fourth, there needs to be a pyramid system in place to designate levels of power, achievement, and authority.

"The following point is a continuation of baiting Christians into feeling the need to earn their way to salvation. These pyramidal levels then become proof of having earned a position closer to god. The higher one of them climbs, the greater their prestige. After all, the harder they work to be close to their cult leader, the closer they are to god."

The previous words vanished, and a new phrase took their place.

Fifth, the cult leader's word is final.

"Not much to add. The cult leader's word will be venerated above the Bible."

Shooting at the board again, the sixth point appeared for Durrell.

Nails from Bullets

Sixth, followers will be taught they will be persecuted for their faith.

He fidgeted. As much as he enjoyed his job, he needed a break. "Cult leaders revel in this ultimate sacrifice. The suffering of their followers confirms they have found the one true faith. Standing firm in their cult provides their self-inflicted badge of courage. They rejoice in defying what they believe are the false gods. It almost seems that some followers are looking for victimization so they can demonstrate their spiritual fidelity to the end, a persecuted death."

Heaving a sigh, the Chief Demon waved at the board where the last principle splattered into view.

Seventh, all followers will be sequestered.

"Okay, students, here is the final point. Cult leaders will require their followers to either be sequestered to a private local to further isolate and brainwash them, or will force them to attend a church that only they may enter since only they understand its icons and rituals."

Durrell sat on the edge of the stage, and asked, "Are there any questions?"

A student along the wall coughed. "Um, sir, I know these types of Christian cults exist all over America and in the Middle East. I bet the agents who influenced the establishments of the big ones must be sitting in the same room with Satan."

The Chief Demon sprang to his feet. "Emphatically not."

Shrinking behind another initiate, the student stammered, "Why?"

"For many reasons. First, the cults flourishing in America tend to get publicity. Along with the publicity, notoriety."

"Isn't that good?" The student seemed to be gaining confidence. And stepped forward.

Durrell stomped his foot. "No. The publicity draws people to the cults, thereby increasing potential targets for our dark intentions. Not to mention all the followers in successive generations who accept the cults' teaching without asking questions."

Satisfied, the student returned to his place.

Man Prefers a Complicated Lie Over the Simple Truth

"Class, this is what really happens. Yes, it's true that we garner many souls, but there's an inherent detractor. People in these larger groups become concerned, study their Bibles and gain more knowledge. The Christian churches begin to understand the true concept of grace. Many members who we would have seeded to hell, grow a stronger faith. Then they realize that although they think the cult is wrong, they acknowledge there are many good people in the cults. Now we really have a problem. Churches stop condemning and hating them, and instead show love and compassion, just like Christ modeled. The end result is we lose possible members for hell. All because Christians gain a better understanding of grace."

Durrell clasped his hands behind his back. Head down, he stepped to the edge of the stage. After a while, he looked up. "Added to this loss, cult members study the Bible more, ask questions which can't be Biblically answered. Their greater understanding of the Bible causes some in the ranks to leave the cult. Now we have lost exponentially. Not only do we lose them, but the following generations too. You demons need to consider the big picture—what happens over the centuries, and how each generation we lose results in successive generations transferring their allegiance to the other side."

He tapped his head. "Remember this principle. When people study their Bibles, they develop a faith for themselves which they then teach to their children and their children's children. Since their faith is built on God and not on another person, they weather spiritual storms, and, this is vital, they don't quit their churches. Do you understand why, class?"

"No." Again, a unified response.

"People can't quit people. They can quit Christian cults, but the true church is made up of living, breathing human beings. Now do you see the problem?"

"Yes, Durrell."

Ah, a well trained class, indeed.

"Now, let's talk about the Middle East. Allowing the biggest cult to thrive in that part of the world was the worst mistake we ever made. You can rest assured the demon who nurtured its founder is serving time in hell right along with him."

Pointing to a student in the middle of the front row, the Chief Demon asked, "Do you understand why?"

"No, sir."

"Look at what has happened since this Middle Eastern cult began over a thousand years ago. They may have millions of followers whose souls we own. Sure, we want this cult to continue because it's an easy way for us to claim souls, generation after generation. However, we have to consider its influence on Christians. Divisions within the Christian faith are overcome. All Christian belief groups study their Bibles more and unite against a common cause. They become stronger, and as their faith in Jesus deepens, many of them stop wanting to destroy this Middle Eastern faith."

Durrell jabbed his index finger at his audience. "Instead, they seek to convert the followers with love and compassion. The more Christians these people in the Middle East murder and martyr, the stronger Christianity becomes. We might gain a few souls during some of the fighting because both sides are filled with hatred, but in the long run, over hundreds of years, all the persecution does is revive New Testament Christianity."

He surveyed the class, searching for a likely pawn. A soul to his left seemed surprisingly intelligent. He pointed and said, "You, what do we learn from this poor example?"

Puffing out his chest, the student drew in a big breath. "We want cults no one has heard of or cares about. We want small cults scattered all over the world, in groups of only several hundred. We don't want them to draw attention to themselves by seeking publicity. We want cults that live and work under the radar."

Durrell applauded. "When did you become so smart? Okay, class. I'm going to give you three very important points. Take note."

He approached the chalkboard, raised his hand, and without touching the surface, sentence after sentence flowed in fancy calligraphy.

1. It's better to go about your work of collecting souls for Satan by getting your cult leader to quietly work in the background

of human society. Don't allow him to draw attention to his work of reaping souls for Satan.

2. Do your best to manage the egos of your cult leaders. Don't let them get out of hand. Otherwise they start believing the lie they have been spreading.

3. Belief in the cult has to incorporate the same type of belief humans have for Christ. They must know, deep within their hearts they are right, and not be coerced by force or fear.

16

Comfort, Convenience, Complacency, and Indifference

After a rest of millennia, or a few minutes, Durrell faced his students, but jabbed a finger over his shoulder toward the board behind him. Four words glowed in fluorescent chalk.

Comfort
Convenience
Complacency
Indifference

"Does anyone care to inform us why these words are so important?"

No one in the room spoke.

"Okay, you waste of evil spirits. I'll tell you. You must remember these four words when you recruit souls for our Master. They will be like keys to unlock and open the door into the heart of each target soul you hunt for our Lord of Death. There are four paths you can take, yet you only need one to steal his soul. If you try one and it doesn't work, then you have three more with which to experiment. Keep using each key, no matter how many times you attempt to unlock the door to his soul. Eventually, you will find the one that is appropriate for the time and circumstance. Remember we are not bound by time so what is thirty or forty, even fifty years?"

Durrell nodded to a student in the front row. "What is the first key?"

"Um, comfort, sir."

"Correct. We encourage the living to become spiritually lukewarm. We promote mediocrity by making them believe lukewarm

Comfort, Convenience, Complacency, and Indifference

is satisfactory. They are not bad people, nor are they lazy or cruel. Most of the times they have good educations, jobs, homes, children, and attend church. In their minds they are good people."

The same dark spirit who answered previously, asked, "Then how are they recruited if they have all this goodness in their lives?"

"Christianity is not about being good. Remember this truth as it is the foundation upon which our stair-step strategy for recruiting souls works. If goodness was all that was required, then you and I would be out of a job, well, almost out of a job."

The Chief Demon set his hands on his hips. "Keep in mind that salvation is by faith, grace, and mercy through the blood spilled on the cross over two thousand years ago. Jesus died as a sacrificial lamb making it possible for his blood to cleanse mankind's sins. Hence, works are not about proving anything. Works are about responding through gratitude for what was done to free men from his sins. No human effort is worthy enough to repay Christ because if a human life is invaluable, how much more so the life of the Son of God."

Durrell clutched his chest. What was that? Not again. God's Holy Spirit hovered over him. He was undone. His fingers seemed to act on their own and wrote on the board.

James 2:19 "You believe that there is one God. Good! Even the demons believe that—and shudder."

His bones seemed to lose their rigidity. He crumbled to the stage, twitching violently, his limbs shooting out in all directions. Durrell knew Satan was in control of his body. Why was he being punished now? He had not chosen to write that verse on the board.

The seizure subsided. Durrell gasped in air and lay still.

Whispers from the class roused him. He sat up and wiped his brow. Whew, that was close. He should know by now his Master was impulsive and exacting.

Jumping up, he paced the stage. What had he been saying? He mentally reviewed the points of his lecture. Salvation. Works. Jesus' blood. Ah, yes. He remembered.

He deliberately raised his voice to show he was in control. "Let me give you an example of mercy. Governors or the President can pardon a condemned criminal. Can a freed criminal, once sentenced to death, repay a governor or the President for his pardon?"

The class responded, "No."

"Why not?"

A voice from the back bellowed, "There is nothing more valuable than a human life. Therefore, the pardoned criminal has nothing to give. All he can do is be grateful for the results of his pardon. Because a man, once condemned, now lives. He was scheduled to be executed but the pardon freed him from the executioner. Grace absolved him from the consequences of his sin and not the act of his sin. He is still guilty of the sin he committed, but the pardon removed its stain. In God's eyes the burden of his sin is washed away by Christ's blood."

"Exactly." Durrell pumped his fist in the air. "I like your style. But I digress. Our goal is to be that whisper in his ear, the thought that runs through his mind while driving to work. 'I'm a good person. I go to work every day, I pay my bills on time, I have a college fund for my kids, I don't cheat on my wife—well there was that one time. I see my family as much as possible, and I go to church at least a few times a month, except when we don't like the preacher, or plan a trip out of town. I give money from time to time to the church. I may drink a little too much, and my kids are good and everyone in our family seems happy.'"

All of a sudden, a large wooden stool appeared on the stage. Slumping over to it, Durrell sat with a sigh. "About time. I'm getting tired. Okay, class, I've just described the first C. This man is comfortable and content. His comfort and contentment are bound up in his belief that all these actions prove he's a good man."

He slapped his thigh. "This is just where we want him. Encourage him to not think any further than his personal comfort. A human usually wants to employ what he does on a daily basis to define his faith. He doesn't want it defined by the blood of Christ. And the more you can influence him to focus on his own goodness and less on Christ's blood, the weaker his faith becomes. In his comfort and contentment, he can look around and compare this life to people around him. They don't do the same good things as

Comfort, Convenience, Complacency, and Indifference

he does, or their morals are somewhat less than his. Again, he is defining his faith by the wrong standard. You must gently nudge him to continue in this direction. The longer he sees himself in this light, the easier your job, and we are home free. All we have to do is wait until he grows old and dies."

One of the new demons raised his hand and asked, "If being good is not enough, then how can anyone get to heaven?"

"Focus on the big picture. Remember when we talked about *deeds* earlier?"

Students nodded, and one responded, "Yes, it's about earning your way to heaven through acts of good works."

"Correct, you slime buckets of waste. You were listening after all. Back to the topic. *Deeds,* and saying *I'm okay because I'm a pretty good guy,* are two sides of the same coin. History records the ancients could never accumulate enough deeds to prove their worth to God. Whereas, the man of today says, 'Hey. I must be okay. I'm the same as, or better than everyone else. No need to worry, I'm good enough.' See the difference class?"

One student quipped, "Yeah. The ancients worked at proving their worth striving to be perfect, while the people today are satisfied with mediocrity."

"Either way, we catch many souls because they are either burned out and quit since they can never be perfect, or they kick back and relax, as the targets do today rest on their laurels." Durrell jumped off the stool, executed a fancy spin, and highlighted the second word on the board which glimmered in florescent yellow.

Convenience

"Class, once comfort has been successfully implanted in your target souls, the next step is to make faith convenient. Now for you to understand what convenient means you have to know something about Christian history. For about two hundred years in the early church, being a Christian was anything but convenient. They met in cemeteries, under trees, in homes, catacombs, or any out-of-the-way place where they could worship their God without getting caught by the Roman authorities."

Nails from Bullets

He returned to the stool. "During the hundreds of years since the rule of Constantine, we've been able to gradually make Christianity a convenient faith. Once it was institutionalized by Constantine, Catholicism and ultimately Protestantism, became concerned with politics and power. The combination of politics and power with religion has been one of the best types of sabotage we have been able to achieve in the last two thousand years. The demons back then who whispered in Constantine's ear and all his political followers responsible for institutionalizing the Christian church, are now sitting with Satan himself. If anyone among us can escape the second death with Satan, they will."

Clapping his hands, he forced a student in the front row to focus on him.

"Don't fall asleep. Remember what happened to your peers. Now, what is convenience? Is it laziness? Is it the ease by which something comes that requires little to no effort? Yes, yes, yes. Therefore, what was once inconvenient and sought after becomes convenient and unappreciated. The reason the organized Christian faith became this way is found in one word. Sacrifice."

The letters of the words hovered above his head. Students' mouths gaped. How he loved the special effects his power created.

"In the first several hundred years after Christ's death, being a Christian required sacrifice—time, energy, money, liberty, and during persecution, even death in an arena. This is not to say there aren't some places in the world today that sacrifice is not required, but on the whole, the fields are ripe for our harvesting because the Christian faith has become convenient."

"Please, sir, Durrell, explain what you mean in more detail." The demon recruit Durrell had admonished earlier seemed eager to get back in his good graces.

"Look for the people I previously described. Those who feel they are not as bad as some, but perhaps not as good as others, but feel comfortable in their lukewarm faith. Remove from their faith the concept that sacrifice is its foundation. Make it inconvenient to attend church services all the time, or to block out time for daily reading of the Bible, and prayer. When they do attend services, make their experience inconvenient. They didn't like the color of the carpet, or temperature in the auditorium was too hot or too cold. There are many other inconveniences you can whisper into their hearts and souls. Be creative and look for every opportunity."

The last two words on the board wavered and then left the board and danced on either side of Durrell's head.

Complacency and Indifference

He waved to the words as if they were alive. They swept back to their position among the others. "Here we go, advanced class, you are ready for the last presentation on how to use human nature against the Christian faith. These two principles, complacency and indifference, belong together because once your targeted Christian soul is complacent, it will become indifferent. In order to reach these last two steps, comfort and convenience must be in place first."

Stifling a yawn, the Chief Demon continued. "These two principles are the final goals of all our hard work. Like I said earlier, it may take you years to help guide your human to no longer care about his faith. But victory tastes sweet and there's no greater feeling than watching a soul fall down into death knowing you are the one who brought him here. It's cathartic."

He raised his eyes to the ceiling and grinned. "Ah, yes. We're almost done. What do complacency and indifference look like? I can't give you any tangible examples, because these concepts concern observable behaviors. In the last several decades we have had other agents working very hard to break down the family. We have been successful globally, but most recently in the United States. There are more divorces than marriages. There are more people living together than getting married. We have a breakdown of the family unit so that marriage is no longer between a man and woman. There have been several places in America where polygamy has been practiced for decades. Murders are rampant in certain cities. Abortion and selling of human fetuses has been going on for years."

Nails from Bullets

Durrell hopped off the stage and paced in front of the class. "That concludes this section of your training. Let's take a five-minute break."

Using his powers, he erected an opaque wall between himself and the students. Although he relished his assignment, he needed a drink.

> "Hear, O Israel: The Lord our God, the Lord is one. Love the Lord your God with all your heart and with all your soul and with all your strength. These commandments that I give you today are to be upon your hearts. Impress them on your children. Talk about them when you sit at home and when you walk along the road, when you lie down and when you get up. Tie them as symbols on your hands and bind them on your foreheads. Write them on the doorframes of your houses and on your gates."
>
> DEUT 6:4–9

17

How to Win Adolescent Souls

Durrell stretched and the souls he'd swallowed rumbled in his torso, pushing against his skin. The students closest to him grimaced. He grinned. There was no end to the disgusting sights in store for them.

He squirmed on the stool to get comfortable. "We're almost done, class. There is one more group of souls you will target in earnest. We have established a special unit to work with teenagers. So far, they have been very successful by focusing on evil and calling it light. For example, teens know more about werewolves, witches, and vampires than they know book chapter and verse in their Bibles. For instance, I'll quote Isaiah 5:20. 'Woe to those who call evil good and good evil, who put darkness for light and light for darkness, who put bitter for sweet and sweet for bitter.' This population is ripe for harvest since they are already mentally prepared to embrace our ways. And my favorite tactic is all the tattoos and piercings that have become all the rage."

"How does this create complacency and indifference?" asked a new demon standing against the wall.

"Parents do little to nothing about their children embracing secular evil. You have to examine this strategy as used in history. It has taken us seventy years since World War II to persuade the population in a direction where they are indifferent. They either can't or won't see that all of the innocent dabbling in evil creates a whole new generation of idols which all have one focus. They worship what is created rather than the creator. Only two generations or so ago, if any of these new trends had emerged, they would have been crushed by parents. Not anymore. Parents want to be accepted by their kids and don't want to seem closedminded. They want to be their friends and not their parents. Hence, secular humanism has become the new idol, and its tenants are the new Bible of complacency and indifference."

"But Durrell, how can tattoos and ear piercings lead to idols?" one of the demons asked. "That sounds judgmental and self-righteous."

Durrell flew off the tool and whooped around the stage. "You hit the buzz words. These are the very words used to justify indifference. People are afraid to stand up for anything anymore because they don't want to be seen as not politically correct, which is another tool of indifference. Therefore, they stand for nothing." He sat again, slapping his thighs. "Isn't it exciting. We don't have to do anything except make them feel guilty for wanting to stand up for what they should support. Do you see the paradox? We have made them feel guilty for wanting to do the right thing. Oh, how I love this work because it brings so many souls to our Master's eternal home."

He closed his eyes and envisioned how proud Satan would be of him. The buzz from the students recalled him to his job. "But back to the question of tattoos. Have I not told you to read your Bibles? You will be more successful in winning souls for eternity's gloom by using the very document Christians use to follow their God. Read my children, read."

Pointing to a student close by, Durrell said, "Read Deuteronomy 18:10–12."

The dark soul quickly found the scripture. "Let no one be found among who sacrifices his son or daughter in the fire, who practices divination or sorcery, interprets omens, engages in witchcraft, or casts spells, or who is a medium or spiritist or who consults the dead. Anyone who does these things is detestable to the Lord."

"If you paid attention to those verses, you will see that God equated child sacrifice to the same form of evil as sorcery. I bet many parents would be horrified if they read those words. Even if they did, they'd want to remain friends instead of setting boundaries for their permissive kids. Their attitude makes our job easier. Hey, you," Durrell said to the next student, "read Leviticus 19:26 and 31."

In a loud, booming voice he read, "Do not practice divination or sorcery. Do not turn to mediums or seek out spirits, for you will be defiled by them."

"I'll read the next one." A Bible appeared in Durrell's lap. "Turn to Leviticus 20:6. 'I will set my face against the person who turns to mediums and spiritist to prostitute himself by following them and I will cut m off from his people.' If you really want to know how strongly God whom we hate felt about dark practices, read what he told Israel to do with people who practiced them. Next, Leviticus 20:27 'A man or woman who is a medium or spiritist among you must be put to death. You are to stone them; their blood will be on their own heads.'"

"I'm tired of reading." The Chief Demon nodded to a short, squat student to his left. "You, read Leviticus 19:28."

The dark soul fumbled with the pages, and finally found the scripture. "Do not cut your bodies for the dead or put tattoo marks on yourselves. I am the Lord."

"These words are—"

"But Durrell," the fat student ventured a step forward. "What have the practices we've read about got to do with idols?"

"Everything." Durrell jumped off the stage and towered over the short student who trembled. "You see class, when these slimy things called human mark their bodies, they start worshiping themselves."

Another student said, "I don't understand."

"Focus my children. Why do humans mark and pierce themselves? You numskulls. To draw attention. During the past few decades as young people have decorated themselves with tattoos, the more they focus on their own bodies. They don't realize they can't worship God and themselves simultaneously."

Plopping on the edge of the stage, the Chief Demon set his elbows on his knees. "But as I said before, humans have to worship something in addition to themselves, so they turn to the dark forces. Mostly out of rebellion, defying their parents and conventional society. There is nothing more powerful in catching souls for our Master than allowing the youth to follow their natural inclinations. It's brilliant. It's magnificent. We do nothing but sit back and let them rebel, and the parents won't do anything because they are afraid of being labeled narrow-minded. Hence, we get another two for one. We get the parents for having no backbone, and the kids for doing what comes naturally."

Durrell lay back, set his hands behind his head and sighed. His passion for evil surged through his body. Ah, it felt so good.

Finally, he sat up and asked, "Are there any more questions?"

Nothing but silence.

"Before we can graduate you as fully capable demons who will encourage mankind to follow his own inclinations right down the garden path to hell, we have one more tutorial."

Knowing what was coming next, Durrell chuckled as anticipation tickled his innards.

"We are going to send you back to earth and let you practice what you have learned. At the end of this field exercise you will know if you've passed or failed."

Short and squat stepped forward. "Sir, how do we know if we pass or fail?"

Durrell stamped his feet, barely able to contain his excitement. "You each have to win a soul for our Master. Those who succeed, will become permanent field agents. Those who don't, will be cast into the Lake of Death and Fire." His roars of laughter bounced off the ceiling.

Some students moaned, while others fidgeted, as if anxious to begin their on-the-job-training.

"Now class, proceed to earth where we want you to listen in on a conversation between a wounded soldier and what they sarcastically refer to as a Sky Pilot, or military Chaplain. Pay close attention so you can better understand the mindset of God."

"Ugh." Durrell growled. "Just the thought of all that goodness makes me sick to my stomach."

> "Do not store up for yourselves treasures on earth, where moth and rust destroy, and where thieves break in and steal. But store up for yourselves treasures in heaven, where moth and rust do not destroy and where thieves do not break in and steal. For where your treasure is, there your heart will be also."
>
> MATT 6:19–21

18

Sky Pilot

While in paradise, Steve watched in amazement all that was going on in hell. Death and Hades served as a training ground to steal human souls? The experience provided him an understanding of heaven and hell. This war between Satan and God was real.

God appeared beside Steve and asked, "Anything on your mind, son?"

"I had no idea our souls were a battle ground."

"How could you know until you arrived here? Now you can appreciate why we care about each of our children, no matter their nationality. Satan makes our children's lives tough enough without war. During combat, they are hurt in so many painful ways—bullets are only one method. While involved in human hostilities, our children are subjected to Satan's desire to entice them to act less than animals. When our sons and daughters have to kill or be killed, their souls are damaged, which is advantageous to Satan but not to me. It's no wonder so many soldiers never fully recover from their experiences, and those that do, are never the same."

God paused and seemed to weigh his words. "It hurts us to see marriages end in divorce, and families' lives destroyed by addictions. My heart breaks to see wives and children abused, and the ravaged lives of veterans torn apart by their broken hearts."

Time swirled by, and God then whispered, "I'm going to let you in on a little secret."

Astonished, Steve sought the essence of God, but only experienced a soft breeze. "You're going to confide in me?"

"We cry." God's words were filled with tenderness.

The medic couldn't believe he'd heard correctly. "What did you say, Father?"

"Yes, we cry. What makes you think we wouldn't?"

"But, you're God. God can't cry."

"Why not? Do you recall the words in John 11:35? I'll remind you. The Apostle wrote, 'Jesus wept.'"

Steve scratched his head. "I remember, although the concept seems odd."

"Just because we cry doesn't take away our power or glory. Our human qualities enhance our omnipotence."

"How?"

"It takes a strong person to cry, not a weak one. After all, I made man with the ability to cry. Since man is made by us in our image, then what makes you think we don't cry?"

"I never thought of it that way." Steve contemplated God's words, then said, "But you are spirit. How can you cry when you don't have a mortal body?"

"I didn't say we shed tears the same way our children do."

"Then how do you cry?" The more questions Steve asked, the more confused he became.

"The same way we laugh, joke, tease, and have fun."

"Wait a minute." The medic sat on the ground and shook his head. "Are you telling me you have fun?"

Nails from Bullets

God's laugh resounded through the universe. "Why wouldn't we enjoy laughing, joking, teasing, and having fun? Who do you think endowed our children with these expressions of their emotions?"

The medic smiled. "Of course, all of these sensations came from you."

A deep silence enveloped the cosmos. Steve wondered if God had left, but then his voice soared over him.

"When we see war taking away the joy in our children's lives, we are deeply hurt. In that respect, we are no different from parents on earth. When our children are happy, we are happy. When our children are sad, we are sad. Just like any other parents, our lives revolve around our children." A sudden rumble shook the environment. "How do you think we felt when man crucified our Son?"

Rising to his feet, Steve crossed his arms as if to protect himself from the sorrow emanating from God's voice. "I . . . I don't know. I can't imagine."

"Our Son's body nailed to that cross was part of the war we have been fighting since Satan's disobedience caused us to expel him from heaven. Some men might believe we don't understand war, and blame us for its consequences, but they forget we have been involved in an eternal battle since Adam and Eve were expelled from the Garden."

Thunder rumbled across the universe. Steve cowered. How could he survive being in the presence of the God, the Most High? But he needn't have worried.

The Father continued talking as if holding an every-day conversation. "Let me give you an example of just one person's war with sin. Here, the dark knight and my angel of light are fighting over his soul. I will clear a way where you can watch Frank, a Chaplain's assistant. But remember, Satan watches too."

Without being told, Steve knew the setting was a large military ward in a civilian hospital in Bulawayo, Rhodesia. Row upon row

Sky Pilot

of men who'd been wounded in battle were recovering. Steve was aware of their thoughts. They were thankful for clean sheets, three hots and a cot. And pillows. Most of all, they were thankful for *women*. The nursing sisters, as they're called in English culture, were busy taking care of each wounded warrior. There was something special about a female's way and her fragrance of womanhood that was therapeutic.

In walked a Chaplain's assistant who went from bed to bed to see how he could help each man. He approached one wounded soul, and said, "Good morning. May I sit and visit for a while?"

The wounded warrior sat up in his bed. "I don't mind at all. Have a seat. Would love to pass the time of day with you."

"Thanks. My name's Frank." He pulled a chair up close to the wounded warrior's bed, and sat."

"Hello, Frank. I'm Phil. You know I wouldn't have given any of you Sky Pilots the time of day until I was wounded last week."

Not wanting to be pushy but desirous to understand why the wounded warrior felt this way, Frank asked, "Why? What happened?"

Phil replied in a proud voice, "Up until last week I didn't believe in God. I was an atheist—had been one all my life. But then a mortar round landed in my foxhole, and I only have these few wounds you can see. None of them serious."

Frank's interest rose. 'Tell me about it."

"Okay. I'll describe my adventure." Phil drew in a deep breath. "Me and two other men had been together for several months assigned to protecting an African tribal village. Not much to do, and at times it was boring, but we had to keep our eyes open. During the day, we didn't know who were terrorists. It could've be anybody. The villagers and terrorists all look the same."

Phil rested against the pillows.

"Then one night, mortar shells started dropping into the village from the tree line. The three of us ran for cover, and jumped into our fox hole where we thought it will be safe. We couldn't have been more wrong. All of a sudden a series of shells hit nearer and

Nails from Bullets

nearer to our hole. Almost as if the gooks had stepped it off and measured its location."

He closed his eyes.

"Then wham! Lights out. All I saw was a bright, white light. Next thing I know I'm here in this bed. I asked what happened to my mates. Sadly, one was killed outright, and the other lost an arm."

After a pause, Phil opened his eyes and reached for the chaplain. "Hey, Sky Piolet, both them guys were Christians. I'm in the middle in the fox hole. Why wasn't I hurt? I don't understand why I was spared. You got a degree, can you explain it?"

Frank shrugged. "No, I can't. But it seems you have an explanation. Why do you think you were spared?"

"Ski Pilot, up until I was assigned to the same company with those men, I didn't much care for Christians. But when you live together like we did, you get to know someone. Those guys lived their faith. Never preachy. Weren't Bible thumpers."

A sense of pride settled over Frank. Those two men had won over a soul with their example. He asked again, "So why do you think you were spared?"

"I don't really know, but perhaps God could see the change in my heart and spared me. As to why they weren't spared, I have no idea."

Down in Death and Hades, the Chief Demon howled louder than a ferocious pack of wolves. He ranted and raved. Threw a tantrum like a spoiled two-year-old. He even reached out and swallowed two students—for no other reason than he was angry that one of his dark demons lost his sword fight.

He had already done this once before, at the precise moment Phil turned his dark heart toward the light of God. Every time he thought of that loss, anger grew inside him like a volcano about to erupt. The dark angel assigned to Phil was one he'd trained. He didn't care that his former student received his punishment by evaporating into the Lake of Fire. Durrell's anger paired with his fear of Satan's retaliation. So far, nothing had happened to him, but in Death and Hades, no dark spirit knew when Satan would surprise and punish. It was one of many fears of being close to Hell.

Durrell rubbed his stomach were the souls he'd swallowed squirmed and poked his skin. "What you witnessed is one of the fears we all have down here. We never know how a soul we think we have on our side will respond to personal tragedy. The dark angel who lost the war over Phil's soul had been working on securing that soul for a long time. At thirteen, he exposed Phil to pornography. At fifteen, he arranged for him to have sex with a rather promiscuous cousin while she and her parents were visiting his parent's home. Then his parents divorced when he was seventeen. His father, a pastor, had an affair and eloped with the church secretary."

As Durrell listed the temptations, his mood brightened. "Phil saw his mother go through three marriages that all failed, by my arrangement, I might add. It was one of my better projects. One for which I was given an award by his Imminence, Satan himself." He puffed out his chest. "I have a stuffed human head on my office wall along with my other trophies. Satan doesn't give out stuffed human heads often. Only for exceptional deviancy of which I am of the lowest caliber."

Huffing out a long breath, the Chief Demon shook his head. "I'm angry enough to chew right through the lot of you."

The students backed up and cowered.

"We worked with Phil throughout his life, filling his soul with darkness. Why didn't we see that one tiny, bright spot? Alcohol, chasing women, two failed marriages. We thought we had his soul in the bag." Durrell beat his chest. "That mortar should have killed him."

While the Chief Demon was monitoring his students' field trip, God decided to offer a lesson of his own to Steve, the medic.

"Millions of angels sang the moment that Phil allowed my light to fill his heart. We up here weren't blinded by the darkness in his heart like those below were. They cannot see even the smallest amount of light as we do because they are fooled by their own darkness. We all were praying for that tiny speck of light to grow, because as you know, man has free will. Then those two Christian men entered his life and fed that light until it overcame the darkness."

"You mean you saw all the evil he did and still pardoned him?" Steve asked.

"Of course. We know how Satan works. So we don't condemn a person. Remember, mankind chooses his path. We will wait a life time if we have to. As long as there is the slightest hope of repentance, we will wait up until a child's last breath on earth if need be. Unlike those below, we seek justice, kindness, and mercy."

A glorious bright light filled the universe.

"My son, it's time for you to go home now."

As angels escorted the medic home, the words of Psalm 130, verses 3 and 4 surrounded him. "If you, O Lord, kept a record of sins, O Lord, who could stand? But with you there is forgiveness, therefore you are feared."

> "I spread out my hands to you; my soul thirsts for you like a parched land."
>
> PS 143:6

> "My people have committed two sins: They have forsaken me, the spring of living water and have dug their own cisterns, broken cisterns that cannot hold water."
>
> JER 2:13

19

The Water of Life

Phil, the soldier who survived the mortar attack, recovered, married, and fathered three children. He lived the rest of his life in modest prosperity and peace, however, he continued to endure episodes of PTSD. Other men and women didn't recover as completely because they didn't have his edge—his faith in God. Similar to many righteous men mentioned in the Old Testament, he lived a full, rich life, and had many grandchildren. He then peacefully died in his sleep, and was escorted to heaven where he met God.

At first glance, Phil didn't recognize his surroundings, nor the man with him.

That is, until God revealed himself by opening Phil's heart.

The deceased soldier didn't see a God of majesty and power, but one of humility and respect.

Confused and uncertain, he shook his head. Who was this man dressed in an old dirty khaki uniform? His face was grimy, and he had holes in the knees of his trousers and in the elbows of his long sleeves. Had he been crawling in the dirt over rocks?

Phil could see the minutest details of the man's appearance.

He held a rifle, and wore a cap with the sun flap hanging down over the back of his neck. The flap might have prevented his neck from getting sunburned, but it hadn't shielded his ears. They were burned and pealing, just like Phil's had when he was in Africa.

All of a sudden, Phil realized the fellow soldier was God. His lips were dry and cracked, and although gaunt, his demeanor was one of a lean, mean soldier, just like Phil had been while on patrol. Dirt caked under his finger nails from digging holes in which to sleep. There were circles under his eyes, a result of physical exhaustion.

Phil detected traces of black camo cream streaked with sweat on the soldier's face. His hair was oily and filthy, and, if he probably tasted grit in his mouth from living in the bush. If he was truly like other soldiers, he could feel the sting in the corners of his eyes from the salt dripping off his forehead.

Peering closely, Phil noticed small cuts and bruises under the soldier's clothes. His flesh endured the abuse of running through the thorny bush, falling down, getting up again. The cat-and-mouse game of hide and seek with terrorists was an ongoing constant trial. Safety and coming out alive was measured in the skill of thinking two steps ahead of the enemy. Fatigue, exhaustion, thirst, and hunger were not excuses for rest but death warrants the soldiers could ill afford.

Phil surmised that the soldier hadn't brushed his teeth in a month of Sundays, nor had he bathed. Smelling like the animals blended in with his natural, outdoor environment. Deodorant or toothpaste and other toiletries could be detected by the enemy.

The Water of Life

God then welcomed Phil to heaven, and opened his heart's perception to the length and breadth and depth of heaven.

Wide-eyed, Phil attempted to absorb the magnificence around him. "God, why did you accept me, and bless me so abundantly after I was discharged from the army?"

"Because you chose light over darkness. You stopped drinking out of your own dirty cisterns, and instead, consumed the water of life from my cisterns. And you continued drinking from it the rest of your life. Not only did you refresh your own soul, but you shared my cistern with many other souls."

"But Lord, you know the kind of life I lived. I became a drunk at an early age. I tried drugs to escape my pain. I was unfaithful to many women. And—"

"I know what you are about to say. Haven't I always been at your side, just like I am with all my children? I know about your gambling."

"Yes, Lord, I bet on horses, dogfights. On all kinds of sports. I was a total wreck. I used money that was supposed to go toward our mortgage. Money from our household budget designated for our children's clothes, food, and medicine. I even used our savings . . ."

"I know." God paused, then said in a quiet voice, "You used the key phrase just a few statements back."

"What was that?"

A gentle breeze wafted around the universe. "To escape your pain."

Phil hunkered close to the ground. He remembered the pain.

But God's next question made him sit up. "Did you ever ask yourself why you drank from all these cisterns? Why you encountered deliverance while in your fox hole sheltering form that mortar blast?"

"Yes Lord, it took me half my life to face what I had been running from, to figure out why I chose those cisterns."

"And what was that, my son?"

Lowering his head, Phil swallowed hard. "I thought I was gay, but as it turned out I wasn't. A man molested me when I was twelve years old. The abuse lasted for several months. Later, as I began to discover girls, I became confused. For some reason, I felt attracted to men as well. That's why I excelled in football, baseball, track and field. Why I joined the army and later became a mercenary. But no matter what I did to prove I was a man, I still felt the attraction to men."

"More cisterns." God's voice held no incrimination.

Encouraged, Phil continued. "Nothing seemed to quell my attraction. Gambling was the only escape that helped me avoid what I was running away from. Not even sex with women solved my problem because I still felt the attraction to men. Sex with women confused me more."

Phil expelled a sigh. He could hardly accept that he was discussing his vile life with the God of the universe. "After that mortar attack, I had plenty of time to think while in hospital. I finally realized it was now or never. I could continue to consume water from my putrid cisterns, or I could choose pure water from your cistern. After all, none of the cisterns I used to escape my pain helped."

Did he hear angels singing? Phil opened his heart. "I finally asked myself a question that I should have asked decades ago. Was I gay? I concluded I wasn't. Being confused about my attraction to men was because of my uncle who molested me. It occurred at the time in my life as I was changing from a boy to a man. I was confused because he said he loved me. You know I didn't have a good relationship with my father which helped me confuse sex with love. The love a father should give his kid. I wasn't born gay, nor do I believe any one is. I've concluded it's a choice in life style."

A peaceful calm surrounded him. "Lord, then you came to me like a flood of life giving water."

"Come with me, my son." The dirty, scarred soldier vanished, and a bright essence filled the space. "From now on you will drink from my cistern for eternity."

The two walked away, but not into a garden. They tramped over something where only two old soldiers could feel at home. They walked over a battlefield strewn with the remnants of Satan's army of dark knights who'd lost their battle of seeking souls. And,

The Water of Life

as in all battle scenes, they soon disappeared into the smoke and haze from the recent battle, soon to be lifted into heaven.

> "You are my portion, O Lord; I have promised to obey your words. I have sought your face with all my heart; be gracious to me according to your promise. I have considered my ways and have turned my steps to your statutes. I will hasten and not delay to obey your commands. Though the wicked bind me with ropes, I will not forget your law. At midnight I rise to give you thanks for your righteous laws. I am a friend to all who fear you, to all who follow your precepts. The earth is filled with your love, O Lord; teach me your decrees."
>
> PS 119:57–64

20

Enter the Fog of War

"All of you, fan out. Stop bunching together." Durrell gritted his teeth as he pointed to the swarm of dark souls. "Do you want the God whom we loath to have one of his Angel Knights take out several of you with one swing of his sword?"

"This battlefield is so thick with fog I can barely see a dying soul." The trainee's voice whined above the commotion.

"I don't care. Keep moving in an extended line with only a few feet between each of you. Open your eyes and scour this field."

"Where are we?" asked another trainee.

"It doesn't matter. There is always a war somewhere on this planet's surface."

Enter the Fog of War

After several hours of searching, another trainee asked, "Durrell, may I speak candidly?"

"Go ahead."

"All I have seen are vague signs of our own dark knights who lost their battles." He gulped as if scared to continue. But he did. "I don't see one Angel Knight from our most feared heaven."

Durrell didn't want these trainees to know the truth. If a human chose a dark knight, the Angel Knight didn't die, but was transported to heaven for reassignment.

"Keep on looking. You are bound to find one dark soul leaning toward Death and Hades. You need to search for the existing struggles between right and wrong on this battle field."

These trainees moved about freely in the fog of war, watching two battles simultaneously in progress. One was in the human world where men and machines were waging war with bullets, bombs, knives, and bayonets. There were also shouted commands mixed with the screams and moans of the dying. Struggles between individuals heralded crude language, biting, scratching, and gouging. Blood coated everything. Only the victors of each human struggle were left standing. Exhausted, they paused momentarily before the next encounter. Some quickly wiped away the blood of the vanquished on their trouser legs before advancing to engage the next personal conflict.

In the spiritual realm of the trainees from Death and Hades, they witnessed thousands of black and white knights engaged in battle. They were in dueling duos next to each pair of mortal human beings. In place of guns and bullets, morality's swords wielded by the white knights clashed against the black knights' immoral steal, releasing the sparks of a guilty conscience in each human. In some mortal conflicts, it appeared the dark knights were winning, but in others, the white knights were close to victory.

Durrell set his hands on his hips. "Look for the contests where it appears the human's soul is leaning toward choosing us. Apply your skills and weapons to influence him."

The trainees scattered around the battle field, advancing from one fight of life and death to another. In each instance they

Nails from Bullets

searched the consciences of every combatant looking for some signs of moral weakness. When they found a soldier who was fighting because it was his duty, they moved on. This search continued until the trainees discovered combatants who had some deviant, twisted motives that could be exploited.

Once these select individuals who leaned toward evil were discovered, the demon trainees next goal was to begin to influence the raging battle. Using gifts from their master, each trainee planned several steps ahead to a juncture where the identified dark soul in combat would place himself in death's trap. Once killed in battle, the soul was ready for harvest.

Occasionally, some of the trainees made the mistake of identifying a dark soul that another experienced field agent had already marked. These skilled agents remained invisible even to the trainees. They had already seen and plotted just where the individual dark soldier was to die by meeting more than his match in combat. Like a bull being led to the slaughter, they were leading him to his place of eternal sacrifice. Sometimes it was so easy, like reeling in a large tuna in deep sea fishing.

When these encounters occurred, the trainees backed off and apologized, and went in search of a new dark human soul. However, there was always some hothead who thought he knew better. He challenged the veteran field agent, and tried to steal his intended slaughter. When this happened, the old-hat agent viewed the upstart trainee as an added bonus. Not only would he collect the bounty on the human soul, but as a cherry on top, he'd reap the soul of the trainee as well.

Durrell and the veteran agent shared the double delight of witnessing the loss of the soldier's dark soul, and the eternal demise of the upstart field trainee. The experienced field agent had the same powers as Durrell. He slowly opened his mouth like a large grouper fish and sucked the trainee into his stomach, where many other upstarts were already suffering. What joy to watch it all take place.

Enter the Fog of War

The remaining trainees who witnessed this spectacle that proved there was no honor among thieves, returned to the battlefield.

There was a downside to being a novice field agent who could defeat the experienced agent and take his prey. Had the trainee been successful, he would have become a marked spirit. Just like the gunfighters of the old west, those with reputations became targets for other upstarts. Sooner or later, the newcomer becomes the victim of his own reputation.

It was sad that humans could not see the heavenly majesty and glory of this battlefield, and all others like it. Picture this. Souls by the hundreds, by the thousands, by the tens of thousands were lifted up to heaven. Happiness results from war as those ascending into heaven are being united with family and friends for eternity. Sadly, there are dark souls who disappear into the realm of Death and Hades. It is on these lost souls that God weeps. He did everything he could to extend his hand for them to enter heaven. But they refused.

Such is the verdict of life because a soldier's eternal destiny is a choice—one only each individual can make for himself.

Epilogue

When I envisioned this book, I knew I wanted to present a unique message concerning PTSD. I believe healing the soul is at the heart of healing PTSD. And in order to heal the heart, PTSD needs to be approached holistically, taking into consideration mind, heart, body, and soul. All four of these aspects of a human are wounded during combat. In order to heal all four, the person dealing with PTSD has to begin with his relationship to God. But this relationship cannot be considered in a vacuum. We must also take into account the relationship with Satan even although it may be involuntary. Hence, was born this four dimensional approach to addressing PTSD. However, it was not until I began writing each story, weaving one into the next, that the idea for this book was conceived.

The details of what happens in heaven and in hell as presented in this book are obviously fiction, but at the heart of this fiction is a message.

God loves us so much he will do anything within his power to save us. In like manner, Satan is so jealous of us he will do anything in his power to deceive us. We may not always understand God's will, but we can be assured he has our eternal destiny as his number one priority. Ironically, we do understand Satan's will. His goal is to trick us into falling for his lie so that we will join him in hell.

I pray this book's message has helped the soldier and the civilian along with their families in the healing process over PTSD.

God bless.

www.ingramcontent.com/pod-product-compliance
Lightning Source LLC
Chambersburg PA
CBHW050825160426
43192CB00010B/1893